Coffeehouse Theology

Jim Thomas

HARVEST HOUSE PUBLISHERS
Eugene, Oregon 97402

Cover by Left Coast Design, Portland, Oregon

COFFEEHOUSE THEOLOGY

Copyright © 2000 by Jim Thomas
Published by Harvest House Publishers
Eugene, Oregon 97402

Library of Congress Cataloging-in-Publication Data

Thomas, Jim, 1954—
    Coffeehouse theology / Jim Thomas
        p. cm.
    Includes bibliographical references.
    ISBN 0-7369-0292-9
        1. Theology, Doctrinal—Popular works.   I. Title.
    BT77.T454 2000
    230—dc21

                                                    00-027810

00 01 02 03 04 05 06 07 / BP / 10 9 8 7 6 5 4 3 2 1

To Jack, Dorothy, and G.K.
Thanks for leaving the light on.
Can't wait to see you when we all get home.

Acknowledgments

No person becomes who they are alone. No book is written by the author alone.

Thanks to Terry Glaspey, Carolyn McCready, and all at Harvest House Publishers for having the vision for a book like this.

Few of the ideas in this book are original to the author; most have been borrowed from better minds and more honest hearts which belong to: C.S. Lewis, Dorothy Sayers, G.K. Chesterton, Mortimer Adler, Francis Schaeffer, Ravi Zacharias, Alister McGrath, and Steve Brown. Thanks for letting me color with some of your crayons.

Thanks to A.W. Jackson, Ron Jenkins, Chuck Smith, Joe Focht, Scotty Smith, Scoot Patty, and Sid Wright for showing me how to turn theology into biography.

Thanks to Nancy Schell, who exemplifies all that is good about the word "Mom."

Thanks also to the rest of my family and friends who are too numerous to mention without making this sound self-indulgent and sappy. The privilege of your friendship enriches my soul.

Thanks to everyone at Watershed Bible Study in Nashville for helping me dig a little deeper.

Last, thanks to my wife and best friend for life, Kim, who keeps the whimsy alive and who single-handedly proves the existence of beauty, loyalty, passion, and wisdom.

Contents

Foreword by Steve Brown

1. Did Adam and Eve Have Belly Buttons?   11

2. What Is Truth and Why Does It Matter?   19

3. What's the Difference Between Belief
   and Knowledge?   35

4. How Do We Know That God Exists?   51

5. How do We Know the Bible Is God's Word?   69

6. What's So Special About Jesus?   91

7. How Should We Handle Doubt?   111

8. Why Does God Allow so Much Pain and Suffering?   125

9. What Is Christian Faith?   149

10. When God Asked Questions   169

    Untangling Basic Theological Terms   175

    Bibliography   183

    Notes   185

Foreword

The early church wrote their theology in prisons, on street corners, and in the midst of persecution. We write our theology in academic institutions. Perhaps that is one of the problems with the church.

There is, of course, nothing wrong with theology when it comes from an academy. After all, I teach at a theological seminary, and I need the job. However, I sometimes encounter a dangerous attitude among Christians. It is the attitude that theology, apologetics, and hermeneutics are only for the chosen few who have the intellectual capacity and sophistication to understand it. "Jesus loves me this I know, for the Bible tells me so," someone told me recently. "That's all I know, and it is all I want to know."

While that's not a bad thing, if that is all you know your faith is going to be shallow, your commitment feeble, and your life bereft of the richness and power of what God has revealed to His people. Someone has said that the Christian faith is like a pool of water in which children can play and elephants can swim. It is that. The problem is that many of us, once becoming adults, want to stay in the shallow end of the pool. Paul said, "When I was a child, I spoke as a child, I understood as a child, I thought as a child; but when I became a man, I put away childish things" (1 Corinthians 13:11 NKJV).

This is a book of theology. It is an important book because it covers the richness and the depth of biblical doctrine as it has been articulated and accepted by Christians for the past 2,000 years. But Jim Thomas has done more than write an academic theology. He has taken the truth and given it legs. In other words, he has made theology what it ought to be and always has been when properly understood—to wit, the precious gift of truth given to all of God's people instead of an academic exercise for a few theologians who have the time and the expertise to understand it. This is a theology written where it ought to be written...where people live.

If you are looking for something simplistic, this is not your book. But if you are tired of the shallowness of Christian slogans and the emptiness of Christian clichés, if you want to understand theology and its implications for life, if you want to go deeper, this, indeed, is a very good place to begin. I commend this book to you. You'll be glad I did.

—Steve Brown
Reformed Theological Seminary/Key Life Network

All science, even the divine science, is a sublime detective story. Only it is not set to detect why a man is dead; but the darker secret of why he is alive.

—*G.K. Chesterton*

1

Did Adam and Eve Have Belly Buttons?

The yearning to know what cannot be known, to comprehend the incomprehensible, to touch and taste the unapproachable, arises from the image of God in the nature of man. Deep calleth unto deep, and though polluted and landlocked by the mighty disaster theologians call the Fall, the soul senses its origin and longs to return to its source.

—*A.W. Tozer (1897–1963)*

IN VIENNA, AUSTRIA THERE IS a coffeehouse whose patrons won't allow its owners to update or remodel. Cafe Hawelka is perhaps the most Bohemian of the more than 1,700 coffeehouses in Vienna. Since the 1930s its walls have been lined with original paintings and posters, many of which were taken in trade for food and coffee by the proprietors, Karl and Josepha Hawelka. A couple of years ago, my wife and I visited this historic coffeehouse that for decades has attracted students, artists, and intellectuals as a sort of second living room, a place where they could go to sit and talk, pause and read newspapers, sip hot coffee or tea and enjoy a fresh pastry. For many patrons, there's something sacred about these establishments, and remodeling a place like Cafe Hawelka would somehow desecrate it. The Viennese prefer to honor and preserve this old coffeehouse as a place where you can talk openly and freely about art, philosophy, politics, and yes, even religion.

My publishers and I have called this book *Coffeehouse Theology* in an effort to capture the kind of feeling you get in a coffeehouse, a place which fosters casual conversation about things that matter. In such a setting, we are reminded that if issues of faith are to ever make a real difference in our everyday lives, we must regain the freedom to talk about them outside the bricks and steeple.

For the past few years I have traveled around the country speaking and conducting a seminar I call "Did Adam and Eve Have Belly Buttons?" At these seminars, participants are encouraged to bring their honest questions about the Christian faith and I make a humble attempt at giving them reasonable and biblical answers.

The questions I am asked reveal an intense hunger to find the common sense intersections of faith and reason and of belief and experience. Many people are looking to see if the Christian faith can bring them *information* that will satisfy their minds, and *transformation* that will heal their hearts.

I have no delusions about my ability to answer every question that comes along. I have a few questions of my own for which I've yet to hear a satisfying answer from even the most learned of theologians and philosophers. I try to embrace for myself what Chesterton said about the angels: "Angels can fly because they take themselves lightly."

I began doing this seminar because I felt the church had not made enough of an attempt to meet the intellectual needs of those who were making honest inquiries into the Christian faith. At most Sunday morning worship services you are not welcome to raise your hand, interrupting your pastor's erudite preachment, and ask for an explanation on one of the great mysteries of the faith such as the Trinity, the origin of evil, or the tension between God's sovereignty and human free will.

As a matter of fact, the opportunity to ask questions rarely presents itself in many churches and many important questions simply go unaddressed. Elton Trueblood points to the problem this poses:

> There is little chance of renewal if all that we have is the arrangement by which one speaks and the others listen. One trouble with this conventional system is that the speaker never knows what the unanswered questions are, or what reservations remain in the layman's mentality.

We have people of faith and people on the fringe of faith with unanswered questions haunting their hearts and minds. Is it possible that the church may be guilty of answering questions no one is asking? And not answering the real questions many are asking? Could this be why the church has become irrelevant for so many? If the church is interested in making the message of the Christian faith compelling, it will have to take the time to listen and then begin offering better responses than, "Because that's the way we've *always* believed," or worse, "You shouldn't even be asking those kind of questions!"

The fact is, we live in a postmodern, postChristian world and many spiritual truth-seekers do not recognize the Bible as the platform for truth. In my seminar, I find I have to start further back, dealing with the most basic issues of truth, knowledge, and belief before I ever begin talking about the existence of God, the veracity of the Bible, or the uniqueness of Jesus Christ.

I, for one, think it's good that people are asking questions about issues of faith. I also believe that when we have honest questions we should go looking for the answers, even if it sounds like we are doubting. This is one of the best paths to real learning. If a belief system contains any of what Francis Shaeffer called "true truth," then it should be able to offer persuasive answers to our questions.

This present age presents unique opportunities for the discussion of faith in God. People are more drawn to spirituality than they have been since before the Enlightenment of the eighteenth century. Science, in spite of its great accomplishments, has failed to offer satisfying answers to our deepest questions: questions about the origin of the universe, the meaning and purpose of life, and a hope for human destiny.

Because we are both body *and* spirit, honest people will quite naturally be drawn to seek out their spiritual roots. This longing for something above and beyond our normal daily realities—what philosophers call the transcendent—is evidenced in the heightened interest for movies, TV shows, books, computer and video games, and other media that feature spiritual, paranormal, angelic, and demonic themes. People are simply trying to find a place where their human spirituality can be experienced and enriched.

In our search to understand our spiritual lives, I believe the best solution for us is to return to a basic knowledge and understanding of God rather than letting out imaginations run wild. Once we realize who God is, that He is really there, and He is in pursuit of us, then we can begin to learn from Him, to see what answers He might provide to the nagging questions we have about our origin, purpose, and destiny.

Unfortunately, many churches have lost sight of this simple idea. Somewhere along the line, they shifted their worship and study away from God and fell into one of two modes: 1) *legalism*—focusing on the details and rules of religion and losing sight of the grace of God, or 2) *liberalism*—denying the historical credibility and spiritual power behind the Christian faith. Interestingly, these were the same problems Jesus Christ decried in the religious leaders of His time: the Pharisees with their religious legalism and the Sadducees with their religious liberalism.

As a result of more recent waves of legalism and liberalism, not a few mainline denominational churches have seen people leaving their ranks in large numbers. Rather than recognizing that their problem is of a deep spiritual nature, church leaders and their hired consultants have looked toward a cheaper substitute by trying to copy the success they've seen in pop psychology's self-help movement. Desperately struggling to become relevant once again, some churches have made the fundamental error of replacing good theology with bad therapy. And in so doing, they have reduced worship of the living God to a one-hour Sunday-morning soul massage, a means of making people *feel* better about themselves.

Now don't get me wrong, I'm not at all opposed to making people feel better, but the real answer to our deep spiritual longing is not to go navel-gazing for a psychological anesthetic that will only lead us into an abstract and impotent spirituality. Instead, we should be teaching the transforming message of the Christian faith, drawing from its historical treasure, and pointing out its contemporary significance. The result will be that we won't just make people *feel* better, we will point them to the One who can actually transform their lives and make them into better people.

Theology is the study of God and the relationship that exists between God, humankind, and the rest of the created universe. If the church is going to meet the real spiritual needs of real spiritual people, it will need to reestablish the habit of teaching biblical theology. We need to offer a theology that is understandable outside the seminary on the street level, as well as one that speaks to people on both an intellectual and existential level. This theology needs to answer the questions in their minds and show

how the message of the Bible can be lived out in their everyday, real-life experiences.

The Christian faith is not for an elite or enlightened few. Since the beginning, Christianity has been offered to anyone who is humble enough of heart to understand his or her need for the salvation God offers. As we present the exciting message of the grace of God in Christ, we must encourage people to engage their hearts, minds, and wills in loving allegiance, not to a religion of legalism or liberalism, but to the living God. Then, and only then, will spiritual renewal be born in our hearts.

There are those who predict we are on the cusp of another great spiritual revival. We may be, and then again we may not. Whatever history proves to be the case, I believe the time is always right to revisit the basics, to find those places where verities meet mysteries, where heaven has taken the initiative, leaned over, and whispered to the inhabitants of earth. Where God is neither deaf nor mute, but where He has invaded space-time history and walked and talked among us.

I don't know how you came to pick up this book, but because you have, I invite you to explore with me the truths of the Christian faith set out in the best way I know how—with common sense and simplicity. Just like you, I am someone who has honest questions and a willing heart. In my search for God's truth I've found a few answers. In the pages that follow, I will offer them to you for your consideration, and I'll tell you why I believe you can trust the good news of the gospel of Jesus Christ.

So in the tradition of the Viennese coffeehouses, let this book become a second living room for you. Grab a cup of your favorite coffee or tea, sit down, and see what you think about the Christian faith. And as you read, it is my prayer that God will give you a clearer vision of His truth, a greater faith in His power, and a more confident assurance of His love for you.

- What is truth?

- Is there such a thing as absolute truth?

- How do we know if truth really exists?

- Aren't all truths relative?

- Why does it matter if truth exists?
  What purpose does it serve?

- How does truth affect our daily lives?

- Where can we go to find the source of truth?

2

What Is Truth and
Why Does It Matter?

Our world is so exceedingly rich in delusions
that a truth is priceless.

—*Carl Gustav Jung*

The Big Questions

It happens to all of us from time to time. Has it happened to you
recently? You get in bed, three hours go by, and you still can't get
to sleep. You are alone in the dark, with nobody around to
impress or perform for, no one but you, the four walls, the
ceiling, and the floor. You're lying there, floating on the waves of
the rhythm of your breathing, calmed by the beating of your
heart. And then the big questions surface. Where did everything
come from? How did *we* get here? *Why* are we here? What's the
meaning of life? You toss and turn, and something more rises
up. How can we tell what is right from what is wrong? Is this life
all there is? Does God exist?

These are important questions to ask. And the answers you
embrace to such questions affect every area of your life. If you

embrace the wrong answers, the effects can be quite negative. If you choose to believe what is false, your life will naturally be filled with all kinds of frustrations as you try to work out your life and keep banging up against truth and reality. But if your questions lead you to the truth, you can come to know a deep-seated joy that will carry you through even the darkest night of the soul.

Looking for Answers

Kim (my wife) and I had just returned home from a long weekend on the road. We were both exhausted and a little bit cranky as we dragged our rolling suitcases up the sidewalk still damp from the summer rain shower we had just missed. My mind was fixed on the personal refuge and restoration I hoped to find on the other side of the door.

Ahhh, home sweet home.

I inserted the key and as I turned it, the lock squeaked out a thirsty cry for a shot of WD-40, reminding me of an item still on my "Honey-Do List." I promised myself I would get to it soon but as the door opened, that dropped away as we were enthusiastically greeted by our two little schnauzers, Rose and Violet. They jumped up and down, ran around the furniture in the entryway, "tap danced," and "boogied." If you've ever owned a dog, I'm sure you're aware of what zealous greeters they can be whenever you return from being gone for a few days. While some might find it annoying, for us it's just nice to know somebody's glad to have us back home.

After setting our things down, we gave them the attention they wanted, petting and reassuring them that we were glad to see them, too. Then I headed for the kitchen to get a cold glass of soda. What I saw there was nothing short of shocking.

The ceiling in our kitchen had caved in and the drywall and insulation were hanging like dreadlocks from the gaping hole. It looked as if a Tomahawk missile had landed on our roof, come through the attic and punctured the interior ceiling of our humble little hovel. Rain had pooled on the floor.

After going through the litany of "Why me? Why now?" questions, I collected my thoughts and called my friend Paul, who had some experience with roofing. He generously agreed to drop by a couple of hours later. When he did, we climbed up on the roof to assess what would be needed to fix the problem.

It soon became obvious that the entire back half of the roof would need to be replaced. In just a few minutes' time, I had assembled a shopping list of the essentials we'd need for the job and was on my way to the supply store.

Some Essentials

With any home repair job there are essentials, and for roofing I learned that these essentials include: shingles, galvanized nails, rolled tar paper, some tar, and a hammer or two. The one other thing that must never be overlooked when laying shingles is a chalk plumb line. With this tool, you stretch a chalk covered string across a section of the roof, pull it tight, then snap it so it leaves a straight chalk line on the roof to tell you how to line up your shingles.

Before I worked on my damaged roof, I thought the only reason for aligning the shingles was aesthetic—that it was just about making the roof look good. But Paul taught me that it is much more than that. While you use the plumb line for the horizontal alignment which keeps the rows parallel and makes the roof look nice, you also use it to achieve vertical alignment: to give proper overlap to each row of shingles so that the spaces between them are never exposed. For a good roofing job, shingles must be aligned both ways, on the horizontal and the vertical, and if they aren't, water can work its way into the house and end up destroying your beautiful interior.

So the plumb line is an essential. If you just try to eyeball the surface or throw the shingles up haphazardly, you'll end up with poor alignment, a bad looking roof and, more importantly, one that won't keep you dry.

The Essential

At this point, you may be tempted to say: "That's nice, Jim, why don't you and your friend Paul go host a show on the House and Garden channel? What has roofing got to do with anything?"

Well, navigating real life is a lot like doing a roofing job, in that to do it well we need a plumb line. We need a standard of measure, a means of keeping our lives in line and maintaining a proper balance. Life's plumb line cannot be something we've dreamed up on our own; it can't be subject to our imaginations, our limited perspectives, or our personal preferences. That would be like trying to align shingles just by eyeballing. While that may work for a little while, gradually the misalignment would become all too evident. A plumb line will hold us accountable; it will tell us when we have drifted off course both horizontally in our relationships with others and vertically in our relationship with God.

In the bigger issues of life, *truth* is like that chalk plumb line. Truth is so essential to our existence that without it everything meaningful in life falls apart: knowledge becomes impossible, any kind of mutual understanding fails, even language and conversation become meaningless. Without truth, all the sciences become pointless and justice is reduced to the personal preferences of the powerful or the many. Without truth, human life loses its moorings and our hope for the future dissolves into disappointment.

Absolute Truth

When I am addressing an audience, I will sometimes ask if anyone in the room agrees with this statement: "There is no such thing as absolute truth."

Usually a few hands will go up. I follow with another question: "Are you *absolutely* sure?" The smart ones back out right at this point, but there have been those who held their ground, stubbornly dedicated to the assertion that there is no such thing as absolute truth.

Well, it doesn't make me an Einstein when I point out that the statement "There is no such thing as absolute truth" is itself an absolute statement and, therefore, a self-refuting one. If truth did not exist then none of us could make a statement that was true, not even one claiming the nonexistence of truth.

But the good news is that truth does exist, and universal, absolute truth at that. That's what objective reality is built upon, and it's quite easy to demonstrate since it's all around us. One example: If you go to the top of the World Trade Towers in New York City and step off the edge, it is absolutely true that by the time you get to the sidewalk below you will need a Band-Aid. There is just no question about it.

Ravi Zacharias gave another example: If you step off the curb to cross the street at the same time a speeding bus approaches, it is absolutely true that you and the speeding bus cannot both habitate the same space-time continuum. In other words, it is either you or the bus. It is not both/and it is either/or. This is not a truth that is relative to how a person might *feel*. The bus wins every time.

Windshields and Worldviews

In Nashville we get around 2.5 snows per year. The .5 measurement is how I count the five "balk" snows that threaten the midsouth annually. My wife and I moved here from Philadelphia some 14 years ago, and during our first winter it became clear that people in the South get frazzled when Frosty's favorite weather comes to town.

In Philly, the highway department is well equipped to handle lots of snow on the roads, and most folks aren't shaken by the prospect of a few inches of winter's white lace. Down here, if TV Channel 4's "Snow Bird" predicts even the slightest flurry, they close down the schools.

But the most frustrating part of winter life in the South has to be trying to navigate the roadways alongside people who simply don't know how to drive in the snow. One of the problems is that some Southern drivers don't seem to be familiar with the defrost setting in their cars because they just don't ever have to use it. And since many of them don't own a single pair of gloves, earmuffs, snow boots, or anything filled with goose down, the idea of standing out in the snow and scraping all the ice off their windshield is anathema to them. They scrape off just enough to allow them a small hole to peak through, then jump in the car, turn up the heater, and drive off to wherever.

So picture a few thousand people out on the roadway, bumper to bumper, headed for work in the teeth-chattering cold, their hands white-knuckled at ten and two on the steering wheels, and each one of them poised to slam on their brakes, which will of course send them careening fender first into your car. How well can the captains of these frozen, two-ton torpedoes-on-wheels see where they're going, each one leaning forward, chins to steering wheels, peering squinty-eyed through a four-inch by four-inch clearing in their windshields? Not very well.

Windshields were made to be seen through. But to do that, we have to keep them clear of debris like ice, snow, mud, and leaves.

A worldview is a lot like a windshield. It's the group of ideas and beliefs about life that form a foundation for our thinking, the set of presuppositions we see life through that helps us make sense of the world in which we live. Everybody has a worldview, even if they aren't conscious of it. We use it to assess life, to see where we are going, to see if we are making progress or not, to define right and wrong, and to evaluate other issues in life. But just like our windshields, our worldviews can become covered over or cluttered with the debris of false ideas about reality. False ideas cloud our view of the truth and cause us to fail to see life as it is.

A bad worldview leads us to mistaken ideas about fairness, justice, meaning, and purpose in life. A bad worldview can lead us to bitterness and fear, cause us to feel lost and confused about which way to go or anxious about what lies around the next corner. It can lead a person to make wrong turns in life, to become battered and bruised by problems he or she never even saw coming. With the wrong worldview, we feel like we're on a slippery slope of one bad decision after another, and life begins to feel like a car sliding out of control.

Presuppositions

Philosophers tell us that our worldview is made up of a set of basic presuppositions, fundamental beliefs which inform all our thinking. Built on top of these are our secondary beliefs, some conscious, others unconscious. Acting on conscious belief is like buying a friend some chocolate for a birthday gift knowing that it is exactly what he or she was hoping for. Acting on unconscious belief is like getting on an elevator and pushing the button to go up to the forty-ninth floor. You unconsciously believe that soon the doors will open and you'll be able to walk out onto the forty-ninth floor.

Each of our beliefs is based on a statement called a *proposition*, which asserts that something or other is true. For instance, the proposition might be "my friend loves chocolate" or "this elevator goes up to the forty-ninth floor." Propositions can be one of two kinds: They can be true or they can be false. When our worldview is made up of propositions that are true, we hold a worldview that corresponds to reality, and we usually end up getting our friends the right gifts and riding the right elevators.

In the larger issues of life, a correct worldview means we believe the truth about things such as God, human nature, and the world in which we live. Believing the truth about these things enables us to navigate life with much greater understanding. All of us at times may feel like we're driving with limited visibility, like it's almost impossible to tell what is true from what is false. And almost without fail, that's when the big questions of life start popping up, exploding in front of us like somebody throwing snowballs at our cars that cover up the last little bit of clear windshield.

If we want to keep our windshields clear, it's important to ask a couple of questions about our worldview. These are deep questions, but they are important ones.

A Definition of Truth

First, we must come to grips with the question, "What is truth?" Since this question has been the subject of much debate for centuries by minds far greater than mine, let me step aside for a moment and let you hear an answer from one of the most prolific philosophers of the twentieth century, Mortimer J. Adler.

> For all who think reality exists independently of the mind and that reality is what it is regardless of how we think about it, the definition of truth is the agreement of thought with reality. What makes a descriptive proposition true is that it corresponds to the way things really are.[1]

Simply put, truth is that which corresponds to reality. If I make a statement such as "I am a human being," it's easy enough for you to tell whether that statement is true or false. If I were to claim to be a parrot, you could also assess the truth or falsity of that statement. There is a correlation between these common sense statements and reality; that is, they describe things as they really are, or, are not.

Admittedly, this is a simple example and the discussion of truth can quickly and easily become much more complicated. But let me suggest that just because a clever person can complicate the discussion about truth doesn't necessarily mean he or she is making any progress in finding it. As a matter of fact, I have met many people who are quite intelligent but insist on keeping the conversation about truth from ever going anywhere. In the end, what becomes apparent is that they enjoy the verbal sparring and looking for moral or intellectual exceptions to the rule, usually to the point of absurdity. At which point, I think whoever it was that said "the most uncommon sense in this world is common sense" had it quite right.

In my few years on the planet, I've discovered that when you find you are no longer on the road to common sense you are probably on the road to some kind of nonsense. And calling nonsense by the name "progressive thinking" won't change its nature or usefulness. Progress is only good when one is on the right road. If you are on the wrong road, progress just takes you farther into your own foolish nonsense. Better to stop, turn around, and head back in the direction of common sense and truth.

Common sense tells us that truth exists. As in the example of the person who steps off the top of the World Trade Tower, no amount of "believing in yourself," or believing that "you can do anything you set your mind to," will change the truth of reality. You can sing "I believe I can fly" at the top of your lungs as you soar all the way down the front side of the World Trade Tower. But when you get to the bottom, your singing will come to an abrupt end.

Is Truth Relative?

At this point someone might say, "But isn't all truth relative?" This is a very popular notion these days. There are those who would even go so far as to say that two contradicting truths can both be true at the same time. But doesn't the statement, "All truth is relative" remind you of the statement, "There is no such thing as absolute truth"? Isn't it a self-refuting statement, too?

When it comes to the issue of what can be classified "relative" to each individual, it's important that we learn to distinguish between matters of taste and matters of truth. If I say "pepperoni pizza is the best" and you say, "No, mushroom pizza is the best," we can both be right in one way. We are talking about the way our individual tastebuds respond to two different pizza toppings. These are matters of taste, and they are indeed relative to each person. Matters of taste include things like food preferences, favorite colors, the make of automobile you drive, which bank you use, or the music you like.

But real life is also filled with matters of truth, propositional statements that are either factually true or factually false. If I were to make the statement "God exists," and someone else were to make the statement "God does not exist," it's impossible for both of us to be making a true statement. One statement clearly contradicts the other, so both cannot possibly be true (just as both cannot possibly be false). One of us is making a true statement, the other a false one. Either God exists or God does not exist. In the study of logic, this is called the *Law of Non-Contradiction*, and it basically says A cannot be A and non-A at the same time and in the same relationship.

To offer another example, you and I could be standing in a field with a cow, me on one side and you on the opposite side. You could make the statement, "This white cow has black spots," to which I might reply, "No, this white cow has no black spots." In this situation, we could both be telling the truth as far as we can see it. A cow can certainly have spots on just one side and since I am only seeing my side of the cow (the one with no spots), I could be speaking truthfully about what I can presently see. But I am not speaking the truth of what really is, for there is an objective reality that exists outside my limited knowledge. And the fact is, our two propositions about reality are clear contradictions. Therefore, they cannot both be true. You were right and I was wrong. It's not a matter of taste, it's not relative to how one of us might feel. You have made a true statement and I have made a false one. As soon as I circle the cow and see it from both angles, I would figure out that the white cow did indeed have black spots. That's the way it is with truth. We cannot make clearly contradictory statements and both be speaking the truth.

And so there are matters of taste and there are matters of truth. In matters of taste there is much room for diversity and plurality of opinion. But whenever someone is offering a propositional statement as factually true, it is imperative we understand that if that statement really is true, then its opposite cannot also be true at the same time and in the same relationship. Upon this principle, the Law of Non-Contradiction, all logical thinking is based.

Facing Up to the Truth

I heard a story about how the Mafia was looking for a new man to make weekly collections from all the private businesses they were "protecting."

Feeling some heat from the police force, they decide to use a deaf-mute person named Barney for the job, thinking that if he were to get caught his disability would keep him from being able to confess very easily to the police about what he had been doing.

Well, on his first week, Barney picks up over $50,000. But he gets greedy, decides to keep the money and stashes it in a safe place.

The Mafia guys soon realize that their collection is late, and they send some of their hoods after him. The hoods find Barney and ask him where the money is. But since they can't communicate with Barney, they drag him off to a sign language interpreter.

One Mafia hood says to the interpreter, "Ask him where the money is." The interpreter signs, "Where's the money?"

Barney signs in reply, "I don't know what you're talking about." The interpreter tells the hood, "He says he doesn't know what you're talking about."

The hood pulls out a large gun and places it in Barney's ear. "NOW ask him where the money is." The interpreter signs, "Where is the money?"

Barney signs in reply, "The $50,000 is in Central Park, hidden in the third tree stump on the left from the West 79th Street gate."

The interpreter pauses for a moment then says to the hood, "He says he still doesn't know what you're talking about, and doesn't think you have the guts to pull the trigger."

The point? Not everybody wants to tell the truth, not everybody wants to know the truth, and not everybody wants the truth to be known. For some people truth is a thing to be avoided. Why is this? Often it's because truth shines a light on the way things really are. It uncovers the reality of our flaws and failures. Truth holds us responsible for our attitudes and actions, and living up to the truth takes guts. It takes guts to obey your parents, it takes guts to remain faithful to your spouse, and it takes guts to go to work every day and provide for your family. For some people, the existence of absolute truth might require putting restrictions on what they perceive to be their freedom. Quite honestly, they're right about that. Absolute truth does put restrictions on our freedoms. But fortunately, that's a double-sided coin. Living in accordance with truth also protects us from harm. When a parent tells a child not to play in the street, it's for his or her own good.

Truth Is Necessary

I, for one, am glad that truth exists because truth is what makes it safe to drive on the highway with other people. It's what makes stop signs, yield signs, and speed limit signs mean something. As I drive to the grocery store, to a restaurant, or to work, I believe those double yellow lines hold true authority. When the guy coming the other way does too, we can smile and wave at each other as we pass. But if one of us refused to recognize the truth and authority behind those lines, we'd both be in big trouble.

What would happen if a few individuals within a community decided traffic laws were just traffic *suggestions*? What if they refused to honor the true authority behind road signs? Worse, what would happen if everyone else saw them taking that liberty, demanding their own way, ignoring truth, and they all decided, "If they're going to do that, so am I!" You'd be taking your life into your own hands just to go get an ice cream cone, and eventually there would be an accident at every intersection.

Taking Truth Seriously

It takes humility to acknowledge that there is an authority higher than ourselves. We must be courageous enough to face up to the fact that we will not always feel like living in accordance with the truth.

If it seems that the roof is caving in on your life, maybe it's because you've been trying to live your life without a plumb line. Maybe there's an essential element missing as you try to arrange things in your life.

If you're having trouble seeing your way through life, and you're confused about finding the right direction to go, then maybe it's time to scrape some of the debris off the windshield of your worldview and reevaluate the way you've been looking at the world.

Jesus Christ once said, "You will know the truth, and the truth will set you free" (John 8:32 NLT). You see, rather than being something that restricts our freedom, truth was originally designed to set us free. It's like my friend Duffy Robbins has said: Truth is like the bar that lays across your lap on a roller coaster ride. That's the only way you can get the thrill of throwing your hands up as you crest the top of the hill. The bar isn't there to hold you back, it's there to hold you in, to keep you safe. And that's what truth does.

How Can We Know the Truth?

I heard Steve Brown tell the following story. After having heard one of the genius' lectures many times, Einstein's driver made the comment, "I'll bet I could give that lecture." The next university on their trip was one Einstein hadn't been to before. He felt sure that nobody there knew what he looked like, so he challenged his driver to step up and give the lecture.

Einstein put on the chauffeur's uniform and the chauffeur put on Einstein's suit. The driver went in, stepped up to the podium, and delivered the speech flawlessly.

But as he finished, to his horror, the dean of students came up and asked the audience if they had any questions for the speaker. There was a young man in the crowd who prided himself on coming up with tough questions, so he raised his hand and proceeded to ask an extremely difficult one.

Einstein's chauffeur paused for a moment, took a deep breath and then replied: "That is the silliest question I've ever heard. You should be embarrassed to even ask it in front of your fellow students and teachers. Your question is so simple, I can't imagine a graduate student at a major university like this would even ask it. As a matter of fact, it's so simple, I'm going to let my chauffeur over here answer it"…whereupon he turned the podium over to Einstein.

The chauffeur could have tried to come up with an answer on his own or fake his way through, and he might even have come close to the right answer. But instead, he referred the question to the right source, the one who could get them to the real truth.

In the end, that is what we must do as well. If we honestly desire to know the truth, we must seek it out from the right source. And that source cannot be of human origin because we humans are prone to wield the truth like a club for our own selfish gain. The historical record is in. It's been evaluated, and human beings have shown how poorly we handle something as powerful and absolute as truth. True truth cannot be controlled that way. It was never meant to answer to any one of us. We are all meant to answer to it.

In the Christian worldview, the source of truth is not just an "it" or a "what," the truth is a "who." Truth is embodied in a single, living absolute: the infinite, personal God. God is the One behind everything, God is the source of all truth, the One who holds all the answers. In the end, it is God to whom we must all bow and give an answer for our lives.

If there is true, livable, propositional truth to be found, if there is truth that will give us a clear view of reality and, at the same time, an anchor for our souls, it will come from God. And in the end, as my friend Robert Benson likes to say, "What we are all seeking is not a list of absolutes but The Absolute."

So let's get out our scrapers and brooms and start cleaning off our windshields. Then we'll be able to see God more clearly through the worldview we embrace.

- *If truth exists, how do we come to know or believe it when we see it?*

- *What's the difference between belief and knowledge?*

- *Is there such a thing as religious truth?*

- *Can we really know anything with certainty?*

- *How do we come to knowledge of God?*

- *Can we really know anything about God?*

- *What is the relationship between faith and reason?*

3

What's the Difference Between Belief and Knowledge?

> If we submit everything to reason, our religion will have no mysterious and supernatural element. If we offend the principles of reason, our religion will be absurd and ridiculous.
>
> —*Blaise Pascal, Pensées 273*

Peekaboo

One of the things I like about traveling is getting the opportunity to "people watch." There are so many interesting people around the country and not the least of these are the many wide-eyed toddlers we encounter in airports. On one particular occasion while sitting at a gate in the Atlanta airport, a young mother and her two children sat just across the way from me. One of her kids looked to be a little over a year old. He was a cute little fellow and just full of personality. The minute our eyes met we both beamed with excitement. *Ahhh!* I thought, *someone else who loves life!*

From that initial contact we deepened our relationship by moving into a round of Peekaboo. Peekaboo is a great game. It's so portable and inexpensive. All you need are two excitable faces and something to hide them behind. You can use a newspaper, the corner of a hallway, some lady's bee-hive hairdo, or just your own two hands. And so we peeked and booed a couple of times, laughing out loud and having a great time. But then this little fellow did something I hadn't seen before. He closed his eyes, hung his head down and got real still for about 15 seconds.

At first, I wasn't quite sure what this meant. But then I figured out that he thought if he closed *his* eyes, since he wasn't seeing me, then I couldn't see him either. If it was dark to him, then it was dark to everyone.

But in spite of what my fun-loving younger friend believed, the reality was that I could in fact see him because he was still there. I didn't have my eyes shut, it wasn't dark for me, and I was looking straight at him.

Youthful naïveté cannot eclipse reality.

Superman

Perhaps you've heard the story of the professional wrestler who got on board an airplane and sat down in first class. He was tall, good looking, and muscular, a self-assured man dressed in black leather accented with lots of gold chains.

Once everyone got on board and found their seats, the flight attendant closed the hatch and started down the aisle to make sure everyone was ready for takeoff. When she came to the wrestler, she stopped and asked, "Sir, would you mind fastening your seat belt?" to which the cocky athlete retorted "Honey, Superman don't need no seat belt!"

A ripple of chuckles spread through those seated nearby.

Then she, being sharp of mind and quick of wit, responded with, "All due respect, sir, but *Superman* don't need no airplane."

Clearly the professional wrestler was not faster than a speeding bullet, more powerful than a locomotive, or able to leap over tall buildings in a single bound. He was not the famed Man of Steel he fancied himself to be; he was probably just guilty of buying into what his publicist had been saying about him.

But deluded self-confidence and hype cannot eclipse reality.

How We Think

All of this goes to show that what we choose to believe may not always be true to reality. As the world becomes increasingly interconnected, with a free flow of ideas shared across cultural lines, it becomes more important than ever for us to have a way to evaluate the truth and falsity of conflicting viewpoints. If one person has grown up believing that the world is flat and someone else comes along and says, "No, it is round," it's a good thing for somebody to get into a boat and set sail to pursue the matter further, to find out which viewpoint is true to reality.

If you and I are to be good thinkers and informed people, we should evaluate *how* we think. Are we thinking clearly? Are the methods we use to determine what is true, what is real, and what can be rationally believed valid? And how does religion fit into the discussion of knowledge and belief? Are there places where faith and reason intersect? Do some religious belief systems line up with reason more closely than others?

If we want to determine what is true and what is false in the area of religious belief, we must first understand a little about the process of how we come to know and believe anything at all. Since this can turn into a bit of a brain-twister, you might want to grab a highly caffeinated beverage, sit up in your chair, and get ready to dig in.

How We Know

Epistemology sounds like one of those words you should never mention at the dinner table. It's the term philosophers use to discuss the origin, nature, and limits of human knowledge. Epistemology deals with questions like: What can we know? How do we come to know anything? What is the difference between belief and knowledge? How can we come to know or believe anything with certainty?

The cultural melting pot we now live in brings together ideas and values from many sources and offers some wonderful benefits. But it has also prompted a crisis over issues like truth, morality, and shared values. For example, while most people agree that "family values" are important, there is no longer a consensus in our culture about what the term "family values" really means. And as soon as anyone begins to offer a definition, another person raises up a list of exceptions, usually accompanied by the statement, "Who are *you* to push *your* values on me?" The result is a culture frozen in moral stalemate, impotent to speak with clarity on difficult moral issues like the teaching of ethics in our school systems, how to deal with violent criminals, how to go about eliminating racism, and how to handle issues like abortion and euthanasia.

This increasing moral confusion is an example of why epistemology is such an important category of thought. We've lost our moral consensus because we've lost sight of objective truth on a cultural level. People just don't know what they can believe anymore. And we are quickly losing sight of objective truth on the individual level as well. Every day we read about another example of how someone asked all the big questions of life and came up with the wrong answers. "Is there meaning to life? Are there consequences to my actions? Is there such a thing as right or wrong?" If the answer to these questions is "no, no, and no," who can blame people for wanting to smash and destroy? Who can blame them for wanting to end it all? They are simply dealing with what they perceive to be the painful truth of their meaningless lives in an honest way.

But there really is a better way. According to the Bible, the answer to those big questions is not "no." It is "yes, yes, and yes." The Christian faith teaches that there is real meaning to life, every human life is significant, there are consequences to our actions, and there is such a thing as right and wrong.

As rational creatures we think and form opinions, sometimes consciously, sometimes unconsciously. But as G.K. Chesterton once said, "A man who refuses to have his own philosophy will only have the used-up scraps of somebody else's philosophy." So if we are to take thinking seriously, we need to consider how we determine which beliefs are true. Whether talking about simple things like how much air pressure is right for my tires or complex things like the meaning of life, arriving at the truth should always be the goal. And while macaroni and cheese is a fairly simple meal and chicken tikka masala is a bit more complicated, so too, some categories of philosophy are simple and others are quite complicated. Epistemology can be a bit of both, but it does offer us a chance to evaluate how we think and how we come to belief and knowledge.

Simple and Complex Truth

The story has been told that there was once a football coach at a major university who was trying to get a rather dense football player through a math exam which he had flunked once already. So the coach went to the professor and said, "Professor, if this student can't pass math, he can't play football. And we really need him on the team. Would you please give him another chance?" The professor was supportive of the football program at the university, and so he agreed to test the student one more time.

They called the student in. The professor, now fully determined to see him pass the test, said "I'm going to ask you just one question. If you answer it correctly, you'll pass the exam and can play football." He then asked the student, "What is 2 x 6?" The young man thought for a moment and then finally, he smiled real big and said, "2 x 6 is 12!"

The professor smiled, too. But then to his horror, the coach approached him and pleaded, "Uh, Professor...could you give him just one more chance?"

That story shows us that some categories of knowledge involve simple, logical truth, and mathematics is perhaps the most obvious of these. In spite of the coach's ignorance, 2 x 6 always has been and always will be 12. There are other areas of physical science which deal with simple, logical truth as well. For example, we can know with some certainty that water at sea level will boil at 212° F or 100° C. This is a repeatable experiment that shows little to no variance. We can say we know its outcome with great certainty.

But there are also more complicated truths that most people readily embrace. These include propositional statements from the categories of science, history, philosophy, and religion. For instance, the theory of relativity, carbon-14 dating of archaeological artifacts, the uniqueness of each self-conscious individual, and belief in the existence of God are more complicated truths, but nonetheless truths most people believe with some amount of certainty.

Poetical Truth

In addition to logical truth, there is also what some have called "poetical" truth, which we find more often in the fine arts. This can be found when someone makes up a story which, though fictional, has some aspects of reality to it. There may be names and places that correspond to the real world, but in essence the entire thing is fiction—a parable, a myth, a fable, or a fantasy. While there may be a good moral principle one can draw out of the story, its details are not to be taken as logically true.

Truth in Religion

When it comes to religion, you'll find propositional statements that contain both logical and poetic truths. Some people make the mistake of thinking all religious truth is poetic truth, that it is all parable and allegory, and that it can mean whatever each person might want it to mean. But that is simply not the case. Most religions assert propositional statements of logical truth, and when they do, those propositions should be subject to the Law of Non-Contradiction which we covered in the last chapter.

So whenever we are talking about logical truth claims, even in the area of religious truth, the Law of Non-Contradiction still holds. No clearly contradictory statements of logical truth can both be true at the same time and in the same relationship.

Still with me?

(Now would be an excellent time to pause, take a deep breath, and sip your highly caffeinated beverage.)

Testing the Truth of Religion

At this point someone might ask, "Then how can we really know for sure? How can we test religious truth claims?" I believe we should treat logical truth statements the same way in all categories of thought. By that I mean that as much as we believe the mathematical truth that "2 x 6 is 12" and the historical truth that "George Washington was the first president of the United States of America," we can similarly evaluate statements about religious truth and come to some rational conclusions about their truthfulness.

For instance, if a religious truth claim contradicts an established truth from the area of science, history, or philosophy, then that religious truth claim becomes suspect. Please note that I said an *established* truth as a qualifier. If a religion were to claim that human beings could fly unaided, that religion would have a long way to go before we should take it seriously because it's a well-established truth that human beings cannot fly unaided.

Let's look at a more realistic example. Judaism, Christianity, and Islam all believe that the universe had a beginning, that it was created by an intelligent, supernatural Deity. If it could be proved beyond a shadow of a doubt that the universe has always existed and never had a beginning, then this fundamental truth claim of all three major religions would be in question. But since that is not the case, these three religions have not been proven false on their common viewpoint about the origin of the universe (if anything, science continues to discover more credible evidence pointing to the idea that the universe did indeed have a beginning).

Judaism, Islam, and Christianity believe quite differently when it comes to other logical truth claims, however, especially those about Jesus Christ. Judaism and Islam would agree that Jesus existed and was a moral teacher. They'd even go so far as to say He was a prophet. But they would never admit to His resurrection. Christianity, on the other hand, claims that Jesus was the very Son of God and that He rose from the dead in space-time history. There is a clear contradiction between these propositional truth statements, and they cannot both be true. Either Jesus rose from the dead or He did not. If He did not, then the case for Christianity is greatly weakened. If He did, then Christianity has an incredible hope to offer the world.

What Is Believable?

The way to decide whether any proposition is believable is to assemble the evidence and employ reason. This is the same way a criminal court gets to the truth about whether or not "so and so" has committed a crime. There may be overwhelming evidence which puts the accused person at the scene of the crime, at just the right time, and also shows them to have had proper motive. This evidence might include a gun with the defendant's fingerprints all over it or some other forensic evidence, like a footprint, hair, or blood. Even though the defendant claims to be innocent and there were no eyewitnesses present, the jury may still conclude that the defendant is guilty based on the amount of convincing evidence.

Working together with reason and logic, that evidence can persuade a jury to bring a conviction in the matter. If someone is deemed guilty, the judgment is described as "guilty, beyond a reasonable doubt" or "guilty, based on a preponderance of the evidence."

Someone might say, "Yeah, but that's not knowing beyond all doubt. Juries make mistakes; sometimes the wrong guy goes to jail." Fair enough, but to operate in the real world, on a day-to-day basis, we can't have a bunch of people running around loose in society who we are 99.9 percent sure are thieves, murderers, and rapists.

To coexist in relative peace, when we see something that walks like a duck, talks like a duck, and lays duck eggs, we can indeed come to the conclusion that it is not a mule, it is indeed a duck. As a wise man once pointed out, "We must believe something before we can know anything."

The Difference Between Belief and Knowledge

I was corresponding with a professor of psychology from a major university once, and he confessed that he was wrestling with some of the intellectual and existential aspects of religious belief. He had become a Christian early on in life but after years of working in an increasingly naturalistic educational system, he had come to a crisis in his beliefs. It was clear to me that he had questions on his mind and longings in his heart, so I encouraged him to know that his honest doubts were not a violation of belief, that he was not doing something wrong in God's eyes by asking questions about issues of faith. On the contrary, doubt can be a sign that a person is actively engaged in thinking.

The central issue running through most of his questions revealed that he seemed to equate what we can *know* with what we may *believe.* But they are not the same.

Knowledge, as most people use the term, relies exclusively on observation and experience. It involves raw data coming into the mind through the five senses. Through knowledge we conclude that ice is cold, water is wet, and fire is hot. This data may be evaluated based on other empirical information previously stored in the mind as well, but the instant there is any kind of value judgment involved, you have moved from knowledge to belief. (Knowledge is the centerpiece of *empiricism,* the viewpoint which claims "seeing is believing" and that direct knowledge is the only real knowledge. The weakness of empiricism is that it would have to exclude knowledge of things we cannot taste, touch, smell, hear, or see, things such as magnetism, gravity, wind, electricity, love, hope, justice, or goodness. And ultimately, the principle "seeing is believing" would have to be excluded from empiricism as well, as it is a concept and not something one can "see.")

Belief relies on observation and experience, but it also adds the element of common sense based on human reason. Belief involves raw data coming in through the five senses, which is then organized by human reasoning, evaluated for credibility, discerned morally, and then, in the end, judged by a person's common sense. Belief involves the senses, the mind, the will, and the heart of a person. They work together to convince us that something is true.

There are varying degrees of conviction in our beliefs. These sometimes fluctuate, but ultimately we choose, either actively or passively, what we will believe. Of course, what we choose to believe does not in any way affect the nature of reality. We might very well believe things which are not true. Whether you believe in God or not does not alter whether or not God *actually* exists.

But for the rational person, the goal would be to discover and believe those things which are true, those things which correspond with reality.

Knowledge and belief show up in many areas of our lives. I *know* there is a car parked in my driveway. But I *believe* that love between two people is something that is real even though it is often unpredictable and not as verifiable or consistent. I *know* that fire is hot, but I *believe* that murder is morally wrong.

In the sense in which I have defined the terms, belief is deeper than knowledge because belief involves more human faculties than knowledge does. This does not mean that belief and knowledge must stand opposite and against each other. To the contrary, to get to the truth in a matter, especially matters of faith, they must stand side by side. As Blaise Pascal said: "Faith indeed tells what the senses do not tell, but not the contrary of what they see. It is above them and not contrary to them."[2]

(Take a deep breath and a sip of beverage. By now you may even need a neck massage from a loving friend.)

How Little We Know, How Much We Believe

I was driving west on I-40 between Knoxville and Nashville when I came upon a wall of fog hanging across the road. My senses told me the road came to a dead stop but this data, as read by my senses and communicated to my mind, did not tell the whole story. Beyond the fog, the road continued. I just couldn't see it. If I had judged the situation by the physical evidence alone, I would have come to the conclusion that I-40 came to an end right there. And so, while our senses are usually reliable, this example reminds us that we cannot judge everything simply by the empirical method. Scientific data must be *interpreted* if we are to know what is real and what is true.

The fact is, most of what we think we *know*, we really *believe*. And most of what we have come to know has been guided by the presuppositional beliefs that make up the foundation of our worldview.

Honest Questions or Willful Disbelief?

Have you ever noticed that some people really seem to be on a quest in pursuit of the truth about God while others ridicule the very notion that truth about God might exist? I teach a Bible study called Watershed in the Nashville area. We've been studying the life and teachings of Jesus as recorded in the New Testament book of Matthew. Within those pages we've taken special note of how Jesus responded to people's questions about who He was, about truth, and about God in general. Jesus seemed to have had quite a bit of patience for those who had honest questions, but He showed disdain for those who were willful disbelievers.

That's an interesting distinction for the Son of God to draw. There are those who have real, honest questions and are actually looking for answers. Their doubt is no less real than the willful unbelievers, but honest doubters are inclined to search for and actually hope to arrive at some answers.

A Rational Faith

While the Christian faith is rational it cannot be reduced to rationalism. If it could, it would not be faith but just another philosophy. We would be our own gods if everything were within reach of human reason. As philosopher Mortimer J. Adler has said:

> My chief reason for choosing Christianity was because the mysteries were incomprehensible. What's the point of revelation if we could figure it out ourselves? If it were wholly comprehensible, then it would be just another philosophy.

And that is the point. The Christian worldview contains both verities and mysteries, things we can know for sure and things that simply leave us standing in wide-eyed wonder. Real life is that way too, and this is one of the reasons why I believe Christianity to be true. I accept as a first principle that we cannot know or fully understand everything about God. The finite cannot fully grasp the infinite. But since God has chosen to reveal some truth to us through the writings of the Bible and through the life of Christ, we are not without hope. We can believe the truths of God's revelation to be true.

But the good news is that if we want to get to the truth about religion, we do not have to close our eyes to reality. We *can* and *should* keep our eyes wide open the entire time we discuss religious truths. We don't have to check our brains at the door when we begin to look into the truth about God and the Bible.

Admittedly, the church hasn't always maintained this attitude. In the early part of the third century, when the church was still quite young, there was quite a little stir between some key leaders. Tertullian (c. 160–225) posed the question: "What has Jerusalem to do with Athens? The Academy with the Church?" arguing that those who had become believers should not study philosophy, which would only serve to lead them into all kinds of heresy. He taught that once a person had come to belief, the revelation of God in Christ and the Scripture was all they needed.

Clement (c. 150–215) on the other hand, believed that God had used philosophy to prepare the Greeks for the knowledge that later came through the revelation of Christ. He saw this as parallel to the way God had used the Old Testament to prepare the Jews for the coming of Christ.

As the church grew in its understanding of the relationship between divine revelation and human reason, along came Augustine (c. 354–430), who showed that the task of Christian thinking is to ascertain what is true and make good use of it.

Augustine searched for a balance. He encouraged Christians to take what is good from philosophy and leave behind that which is bad. Augustine struck a balance and taught that we could be discerning thinkers and embrace all truth as God's truth.

You may have heard the story of the four rabbis who had a series of theological arguments, and three were always in accord against the fourth. One day the odd rabbi out, after the usual "3 to 1, majority rules" statement that signified he had lost again, decided to appeal to a higher authority.

"Oh, God!" he cried. "I know in my heart that I am right and they are wrong! Please give me a sign to prove it to them!"

It was a beautiful sunny day, but as soon as the rabbi finished his prayer, a storm cloud moved across the sky above the four. It rumbled once and dissolved. "A sign from God! See, I'm right, I knew it!"

But the other three disagreed, pointing out that storm clouds form on hot days.

So the rabbi prayed again: "Oh, God, I need a bigger sign to show that I am right and they are wrong. So please, God, send a bigger sign!"

This time four storm clouds appeared, rushed toward each other to form one big cloud, and a bolt of lightning slammed into a tree on a nearby hill.

"I told you I was right!" cried the rabbi. But, alas, his friends insisted that nothing had happened that could not be explained by natural causes.

Now the rabbi was getting ready to ask for a bigger sign, but just as he said, "Oh God…" the sky turned pitch black, the earth shook, and a deep, booming voice echoed out, "HE…IS…RIGHT!"

The rabbi put his hands on his hips, turned to the other three, and said, "Well?"

"So," shrugged one of the other rabbis, "now it's 3 to 2."

Like the three overconfident rabbis, some people are just dead set against reasonable discussion on issues of faith. They are not honest doubters, it's more that they are willful disbelievers. No matter how much evidence is presented or how much reason is marshaled, they will always choose not to believe.

In the end, belief does not exclude all doubt, but it does transcend it. The ultimate question is this: Do we have the courage to believe the truths we can grasp and to trust God to be in control of those we cannot?

- Does God exist?

- There are many different ideas about God; if God does exist, how do we know which God is the true one?

- What do atheists and agnostics believe about God?

- Is belief in God rational or irrational?

- Why doesn't God just show Himself to us?

- What is the evidence for God's existence?

4

How Do We Know That God Exists?

Men can always be blind to a thing so long as it is big enough.

—*G.K. Chesterton*

I GREW UP IN A CLIMATE WHERE faith existed but was seldom questioned. After all, when you're a kid adults tell you that Santa Claus, the Easter Bunny, the Tooth Fairy, and God are all real. You are also told that believing in them will get you gifts, baskets of candy, coins under your pillow, and an all-powerful someone who can help you out of any jam. So what kid wouldn't become a believer?

As I grew older, I eventually discovered that three of the four were not *really* real. (I hope I'm not bursting anyone's bubble here.) But what was I to do with the fourth? No one could show me God. So I began to ask questions like, "Does God really exist or is He something that we made up, like a fairy tale, to help us get through life?" and "If God exists, what is He really like?"

Differing Views of God

I'm not alone in this. People have been debating the reality of God for centuries. Their conclusions vary a good bit and have been influenced by a wide number of factors. Even a casual study of human history would show that there have always been some people who believed in God and some who did not. But just in terms of sheer numbers, the vast majority of people down through the centuries have held some kind of belief in a God or god(s). This belief is generally called *theism*, of which there are three different varieties.

Monotheism, which includes Christianity, Judaism, and Islam, is the belief that there is just one God who is the creator and sustainer of everything that exists. Monotheists believe that this God is all-powerful and all-knowing, the only self-existent being. They believe that God is not confined by time and space as we humans are. God has an intellect, a will, and a purpose behind all that He does and allows.

Polytheism is the term which characterizes most religions outside of the three monotheistic faiths. Polytheists include the ancient Greeks and Romans as well as most Eastern religions and Native American tribes. They believe there are many different gods and that none of them are ultimately supreme. Sometimes the gods even stand at odds with one another and battle against each other. The various gods are usually defined by their job description (i.e. the goddess of love, the god of fertility, the god of the sun, the moon, or the harvest, etc.).

Pantheism is the term which characterizes the idea that the universe as a whole is god. Here, god is not so much a personality as a force or energy which permeates the entire universe. The universe is, in a sense, god's body. Instead of having a will and an intellect, the god of pantheism is like the battery the universe runs on. Pantheism thrives in Eastern belief systems such as Hinduism and Buddhism, as well as in the modern New Age movement.

There is a popular notion that all religions point to the same God. I wish I could say that was true, but the fact remains that they don't. At the same time, as a Christian, I don't have to believe that other religions have everything all wrong. But where they disagree, I find I am forced to make a choice.

The most obvious difference between polytheists and monotheists is in their conception of how many god figures exist. Polytheism suffers from a difficulty in language and logic. If by definition "God" is the term that describes a *supreme* being, then God could not be limited by a job description or in any other way. As for pantheism, if god is impersonal, there is no divine viewpoint from which to determine right and wrong thinking. Therefore, how could we ever get to any "right" thinking about God? As C.S. Lewis pointed out in his book *Mere Christianity,* pantheists do not believe in a God "who takes sides, who loves love and hates hatred, who wants us to behave in one way and not in another." And so, from the pantheistic view, we have no basis for moral judgment or justice. Monotheists, on the other hand, believe that God has set specific parameters for right and wrong thinking and behavior. We are not left to guess-work. These parameters have been spelled out for us through divine revelation.

Within the major monotheistic belief systems of Christianity, Islam, and Judaism, there are also some basic disagreements. The most significant of these relates to the central figure of the Christian faith, Jesus Christ. There is disagreement about His mission on earth and whether or not He rose from the dead after being crucified on the cross. While Jews and Muslims acknowledge the historicity of Jesus Christ, and even go so far as to recognize Him as a teacher and prophet, they do not accept the reality of His resurrection or the idea that His death on the cross paid the price for our sins.

Christians, on the other hand, believe that while Jesus Christ did serve in the role of teacher and prophet, He was really much more than that. Christians believe that Jesus was God-the-Son come to earth in the flesh with the purpose of restoring the relationship between God and humanity by dying for the sins of His people.

So, while the three major monotheistic belief systems do have some things in common, when it comes to the atoning work of Christ on the cross as the means of salvation, they are not pointing in the same direction at all.

These differences do not mean that people from these groups should go about hating each other or treating each other badly. As a matter of fact, such behavior goes directly against what most of them believe. But while tolerance is good, we should not make the mistake of equating tolerance with intellectual acquiescence by ignoring the distinctive truth claims in the different belief systems. The paths are not all the same, and we show disrespect to their beliefs if we suggest they are.

Atheism and Agnosticism

Atheists deny God's existence altogether. True atheists believe that the material world is all there is, and any reality beyond the physical realm is denied. The sense of a greater meaning and purpose to life is not a part of an atheist's belief system. You live, you die, and that's all there is. Johann Richter (1763–1825) said of atheists: "No one is so much alone in the universe as a denier of God. With an orphaned heart, which has lost the greatest of fathers, he stands mourning by the immeasurable corpse of the universe."

Atheists don't believe the evidence for God is conclusive, and some even believe that there is evidence against the existence of God. Yet they are not able to offer any reasonable answers to the big questions of where we come from or why there is such intricate order and beauty in the universe. Because any reference to the immaterial world is out of bounds for true atheists, also out of bounds—if they are going to remain consistent—are imma-terial things like love, hope, soul, and morality.

Lastly, there are those who call themselves *agnostics*. They claim that the human mind can never know whether or not there is a God, an ultimate cause, or anything beyond the mate-rial world. For the agnostic, such knowledge is viewed as beyond the reach of our feeble minds.

Joseph Earnest Renan once said that if an agnostic were to pray, the prayer would go something like this: "O God, if there is a God, save my soul, if I have a soul."

Since we are finite creatures struggling to understand the infinite, it's normal and even logical for us to have some unre-solved questions about God. God wouldn't be God if we could know all there is to know about Him. But that doesn't give us the right to become spiritual ostriches, burying our heads in the sand and shutting out the possibility of any knowledge of God. Curiosity about God and an innate longing to connect with Him will drive the honest seeker to want to know more about Him.

As humans we are relational creatures. When we are alone, in the quiet of our hearts, we find that our soul's deepest hunger is spiritual and relational. We long for a connection with our Creator. This hunger could never be satisfied if God were unknowable or if He is only some sort of impersonal force that permeates the universe.

Philip Yancey once wrote that God is not "a misty vapor but an actual Person. A Person as unique and distinctive and color-ful as any person I know. God has deep emotions; He feels delight and frustration and anger." This is the God of the Bible, the God who is really there, the God who wants to be known.

Some complain that though God exists He seems to be hiding Himself from us, as if He didn't want to be found or bothered. On the contrary, as Blaise Pascal said, "Instead of complaining that God has hidden himself, you should give Him thanks for having revealed so much of Himself."

So what is the evidence for the existence of God? How do we know that God exists? In what ways has God revealed Himself?

The Evidence of God

Many things point to the existence of God. But we must bear in mind that we can't *see* God in the same way that we see the moon in the night sky. Because God is Spirit, seeing God will require that we see with the eyes of our minds, our hearts, and our souls.

You and I believe in a lot of things that we cannot see, hear, smell, taste, or touch. We believe in feelings like love and desire, motivations like will power and hope, forces like gravity and magnetism, even historical figures like Darwin and Nietzsche. We believe thousands of things about science, history, philosophy, and religion for which we have no immediate empirical access or proof. So what do we do?

We gather evidence, make use of our reason, and come to rational conclusions. More often than not, however, we rely on the evidence of testimonies of "experts" to believe in things which lie beyond our five senses. A testimony is a witness or report presented by those who have "been there" like astronauts, molecular biologists, philosophers, theologians, or the authors of great books from previous centuries. Sometimes a testimony may come from physical evidence, such as archaeological artifacts, geological surveys, or cosmological data.

For instance, I believe that the United States of America went through a civil war in the mid-1800s even though I wasn't actually there to see it happen. I might not believe in the Civil War if there were only one clue, like a single sword found in a field near Gettysburg. But the cumulative evidence convinces me: hundreds of swords, cannonballs, rifles, uniforms, letters of soldiers, books, etc. There's a mountain of evidence available that supports the existence of the Civil War, so I conclude by way of rational probability that there was one.

Likewise, I may not be able to see God with my eyes or touch Him with my hands, but there's not only a mountain of evidence, there's an entire universe of evidence that supports God's existence.

The Testimony of Curiosity

Perhaps the best place to start our search for evidence of the existence of God is where we are at right now—asking questions like these. The fact that we have a brain which can think thoughts and ask questions is what we might call the *Testimony of Curiosity*, our longing to know God.

Where does this interest come from? What is the source of our longing for God? Why are we so curious about something we cannot experience physically? If we have such a strong curiosity about the spiritual realm it must at least suggest that there is a spiritual realm for us to be curious about.

When we get away from the noise and racket of our own busyness, perhaps while standing at the seashore and listening to the rhythm of the majestic ocean or gazing up into a clear night sky salted with millions of stars, we suddenly become aware that there is something other, something larger than ourselves, something beyond what we can experience through our physical senses. And we are drawn to it by a strange combination of wonder, fear, and awe.

This curiosity also becomes apparent when we are watching something as simple as a spider spinning her web. Which way will she throw her sticky silver strand next? How does she know how to build such a well engineered edifice? Our curiosity is aroused and we wonder who equipped her to perform this task, who taught her how to do these things? And how is her web so beautiful and so well designed?

As magnificent as the ocean is, it is not the thing we long for. Otherwise, we could live near the coast and never feel this longing again. As incredible as the heavens are, they are not what we long for either. We can see a million nighttime skies and watch a thousand science fiction movies, imagining ourselves traveling around the galaxies at warp speed, and still not experience conclusive satisfaction. The same can be said for watching the spider, the beaver, the eagle, or the owl. In the end, they are all just road signs. They point us in the right direction, but they are not our destination.

Can this curiosity ever be satisfied? Is there anything in this world that will fulfill the longing in our hearts for that something other, that something larger and beyond what we can experience with our senses? Or does this insatiable curiosity and longing suggest we should be looking somewhere else? As C.S. Lewis has said, "If I find in myself a desire which no experience in this world can satisfy, the most probable explanation is that I was made for another world." And that is what the Christian faith teaches, that you and I are more than impersonal matter, and we are standing on the outside of a glass door looking in, longing to be reunited with the source of our being: the infinite, personal God who alone can give our lives meaning.

The existentialist philosopher Jean Paul Sartre once said, "A finite point has no meaning unless it has an infinite reference point." For the atheist Sartre there was no infinite reference point and so for him, life had no meaning. It was despairingly absurd. But for those who have come to believe in the God who is there, there is indeed an infinite reference point. And the good news is that this infinite reference point is not just a force or a fog, but a face. The Christian faith teaches that God has personality. It asserts that God is intelligent, can communicate, and can love and be loved. Only a God with personality can satisfy the deep-seated, spiritual longing in our souls to find our source in the universe.

And so the pull of curiosity provides us with a clue about the existence of God. It is as if God has written curiosity into our software that we would hunger to know Him and that we would never be satisfied with cheap substitutes. Sartre was right in this much: We are finite and no other finite thing can provide us with meaning for our existence. Not success, not leisure, not pleasure. Only God has the capacity to fill our lives and give our lives meaning. If we follow the road signs, they eventually point us not to a "where" or a "what," but to a "Who."

The Testimony of Awareness

Another evidence of God's existence is what we might call the *Testimony of Awareness*. This evidence focuses on the human abilities of perceiving and processing information.

One of the things we tend to take for granted is the amazing way our five senses perceive information—the taste of lemon, chocolate, ketchup, or mustard; the sight of rich colors in a sunset on a Florida gulf beach; the smell of hot chocolate chip cookies in one of those walk-up places at the mall; the feel of mud squishing between your toes; or the familiar sound of a dog barking at a pesky squirrel. Did our ability to perceive all these things come about by accident or design?

Each of us has about 26 million olfactory nerve receptors per square inch in our nasal cavities. When smell particles enter our noses, they stimulate a sequence of these receptors which in turn send a message to the lobe of the brain that mediates our sense of smell. As we go through life, our brains have stored the memory of thousands of such sequences. That's how we distinguish between the smell of hot raisin bread and our grandmother's perfume.

This same amazing complexity can be seen in our sense of taste, touch, hearing, and sight. How many different kinds of food can we distinguish by taste? (Peanut butter, pineapple, and pizza?) How many voices on the other end of the phone can we identify after hearing them say just one syllable of our name? How many colors, shapes, sizes, and distances can we distinguish with our eyes? What about our ability to feel the difference between something that is smooth or coarse, hot or cold, sharp or dull? The complex systems of our five senses and the way they interact with the brain (which is far more advanced than most computers) is amazing evidence of intelligent design.

Not only are the systems themselves incredible evidence of God, but the fact that He created us with these systems tells us that He desires for us to know things. Why else would God have designed us to be industrial strength, information gathering, mental vacuum cleaners, able to suck up vast amounts of knowledge about the world around us? God wants us to know about Him. More importantly, He wants us to know Him.

Belief in God has been called "blind faith" by some critics of faith. But with such clear evidence as that found in the intelligent design of our five sensory systems, doesn't it take more blind faith to attribute these systems to some accidental arrangement of atoms in an impersonal universe than it would to believe they came off the design table of an intelligent Creator?

The Testimony of Awareness, our ability to perceive and process information, speaks of God's existence, His intelligence, and His intention for us to be able to come to knowledge about the real world we live in.

But let's look further; there is more.

The Testimony of Nature

Not only are we curious about the supernatural and capable of perceiving and processing information about the natural realm through our five senses, but we also have the testimonial evidence of the very real things that exist in the observable universe around us. The *Testimony of Nature* is another evidence of God's existence.

The psalmist tells us that "the heavens are telling of the glory of God" (Psalm 19:1). Have you ever tried to count the stars in a night sky? Dr. David Block, professor of Astronomy and Applied Mathematics at the Witwatersrand University in Johannesburg,

South Africa says, "If we were to count all the stars in the Milky Way at a rate of one per second, the process would take two thousand five hundred years!" That's a lot of glory to God coming from just one galaxy.

Earth is but a tiny planet orbiting a small star, one of several billion stars in what we call the Milky Way Galaxy. The Milky Way is one of 30 galaxies in what is called the "Local Group" of galaxies which stretches some 10 million light years across.

The entire universe is estimated to be at least 15,000 million light years across and up to 20 billion years old. Consider again the question of origin: Where did all this come from? And the questions of order: Why is the universe so beautiful and well balanced? How could such a complex universe be so finely tuned as to allow for intelligent life on our planet? Science answers by pointing to the laws of physics. But as thinking people we are compelled to ask: So, who established the laws of physics?

In the past couple of years astronomers have become increasingly more confident about the Big Bang Theory and the idea that the universe had a beginning. While the argument for God's existence is not dependent on scientific validation, it is interesting that the more science learns, the more convincing the case for the Bible's idea of God becomes. If the universe had a beginning, then it must have had a Beginner, someone who caused the Big Bang to bang.

The complexity and order of the cosmos point to an intelligent designer, an originator and manager of the universe and all that it contains. Sir Isaac Newton, one of the fathers of modern science, once said, "This most beautiful system of the sun, planets and comets, could only proceed from the counsel and dominion of an intelligent and powerful Being." Nature speaks clearly and does not stutter about the existence of a designer.

Astronomer Carl Sagan, in his SETI (Search for Extraterrestrial Intelligence) program claimed that if we were able to find just one message with information in it from outer space, that would prove the existence of extraterrestrial intelligence. He did not claim that we would have to be able to interpret the information, we would just need to be able to identify it as *information*. That's a very interesting statement when you consider that in the field of biology, scientists have discovered that DNA is more than just matter, it is matter that matters. A single strand of DNA "is so efficient that all the information needed to specify an organism as complex as a human being weighs less than a few thousand millionths of a gram and fits into less space than the period at the end of this sentence."[3] How's that for a microchip? DNA is so full of information, it should silence all doubt about the intelligent design evidence for the existence of God.

The Testimony of Cause and Effect

In the real world where we all live, logic tells us that every known effect has to have a cause. The fact that we exist, are aware of our existence, and can think and reason, all point to a cause. Who or what started it all and brought the very first people into existence? The *Testimony of Cause and Effect* is another evidence for God's existence.

Some believe that rather than an intelligent Designer/Creator, "chance" is the cause and the answer to our questions about origin, purpose, and destiny. They suggest that the universe is the result of a big cosmic accident, and our existence and consciousness can be explained by pointing to a subsequent series of smaller time-plus-chance events dubbed *evolutionary development*. But what is the likelihood of chance being our cause?

In an interesting book entitled *Does God Exist? The Debate Between Theists and Atheists* (Prometheus Books, Buffalo, NY, 1993), J.P. Moreland argues that Cambridge astronomer Fred Hoyle has calculated the chance possibilities of life arising spontaneously by chance to be similar to the probability of a tornado blowing through a junkyard and spontaneously forming a fully functional Boeing 747 out of the trash.

In his book *Not a Chance*, R.C. Sproul quotes French writer and philosopher Voltaire (1694–1778) as saying that "what we call chance can only be the unknown cause of a known effect." That is to say, chance isn't really the cause of anything. When we say something happened by chance we simply mean that we do not yet know what actually caused it to happen. Chance alone has no causal power to make anything happen because, as Sproul points out, chance is nothing. Therefore, it would be illogical to say that our existence and consciousness are a result of chance.

Indeed it's logical to assume that whatever *caused* us would have to be more intelligent and self-aware than we are because something greater cannot come from something lesser. We would naturally expect the contrast between us and our cause to be quite distinct. So distinct, in fact, that we probably wouldn't have the ability to understand even a small bit of who He is unless, of course, He were to take the initiative and reveal Himself to us. And at that point, we are really talking about the Christian God, not just a cosmic force.

So, who programmed you with a curiosity and longing for something beyond what this world can offer? Who designed the hundreds of thousands of nerve endings that connect your eyeball to your brain and enable you to read this book? Where did the "information processing chip" for the million-million plus cells in your brain come from? Our hunger for the spiritual, our amazing capacity to perceive and process information, the magnificent artwork of nature, all of these serve as testimonies to the existence of God. But there are more testimonies…

The Testimony of Conscience

If you peer into a microscope for the rest of your life I doubt you'll be able to find an explanation for that part of human nature which serves as the voice of moral law. The *Testimony of Conscience* is yet another evidence of the existence of God.

As a species, humans have a built in sense of right and wrong, of *should* and *should not*, of *ought* and *ought not*. Yes, there are mild variations within the different cultures and civilizations down through the ages, but these variations really don't amount to much. Murder, lying, stealing, unfaithfulness, hate and abuse of all kinds, these are activities universally acknowledged to be morally wrong. Meanwhile, charity, generosity, respecting others, kindness, and honesty are universally seen as good. You don't have to be a philosophical genius to see that there's a difference between the actions of Mother Teresa and Adolf Hitler.

Where does this sense of right and wrong come from? It hasn't shown up in our blood, our DNA, or our bones. Even if it does someday, who put it there to start with? Conscience is not a simple animal instinct that we are compelled to obey like some wild dog protecting its turf.

Some have tried to dismiss this inner moral law by saying that moral truth is relative—"what's right for you is what's right for you and what's right for me is what's right for me." But the logical outcome of this kind of thinking is moral anarchy. Any culture based on it is surely on its way to collapse because we humans can be such a selfish lot. What if I wake up one morning and decide that what's right for me today is that I come over to your house and steal your computer, take your wife, or paint your house fluorescent pink? Moral relativism just won't work when it comes to living in a society of more than one.

Doesn't it seem likely that the same designer who placed Orion's belt in the sky has blessed us with a sense of right and wrong which gives balance to our existence together on earth. Instead of creating us as preprogrammed robots that could only do good, God reveals His moral law as something we can understand as well as be responsible to. We have the choice of obedience or disobedience, which we must make on a moment by moment basis.

At times we've all tried to avoid or deny the moral law, especially when obeying it will cost us something. Other times we are quick to appeal to it, usually when it's convenient or beneficial to us. In arguments with other people, we often depend on moral law when we protest, "That's not fair!" In order to claim that something is "not fair," we have to first acknowledge the existence of a universal way to measure *fairness*. Once we acknowledge that, we are back at moral law. The existence of this universal moral law points us toward God. We simply cannot have something like moral law without a moral lawgiver.

But unlike the physical laws of our universe which are compulsory (you can only ignore the law of gravity at your own peril), the moral law is optional. We cannot continue to live without breathing air but we can and will both obey and disobey our consciences daily. With it we manage the health and welfare of our souls, for the good or for the bad, by the choices we make. Each and every time we make a bad moral choice, we harden our hearts. Soon we are no longer tender to the voice of our conscience.

Søren Kierkegaard saw the conscience as our *connector* to God when he said:

> A man could not have anything upon his conscience if God did not exist, for the relationship between the individual and God, the God-relationship, *is* the conscience, and that is why it is so terrible to have even the least thing upon one's conscience, because one is immediately conscious of the infinite weight of God.

Cumulative Evidence

These are only a few of the arguments that point to the existence of God. Of course, none of these arguments by themselves prove the existence of God. But together these arguments serve as clues that all point to God's existence. Just as in the case of the historicity of the Civil War and almost everything else we have come to believe, it is the weight of the cumulative evidence that leads us to a logical conclusion that something is real.

I'd also like to add that the existence of God is not dependent on whether you or I believe. If God does exist, He exists whether we believe it or not. And if God exists, He exists not "however you understand Him to be," but as He is in reality. If God is the very source of all real things, then God must be more real than anything else. Our inability to comprehend very much about God is not proof that He doesn't exist. Rather, it is proof that He exists and goes far beyond our limited concept of reality.

The Testimony of My Life

Lastly, I'll share with you from my own experience. I came to believe in God at a young age and then later went through a time of questioning. Partly as a result of becoming disenchanted with the church, and partly as a result of an honest hunger to know what was true about God, I began reexamining the basics of Christian faith. At times, belief in God and the act of going to church struck me as a Pollyannaish "leap of faith" because it seemed like a lot of people around me had accepted the Christian faith blindly. Instead of coming to an intelligent decision about something that was objectively true, faith seemed more like a default setting for anyone born into our culture. You believe in God, you go to church. But there I was with questions I knew science couldn't answer, and I wasn't sure if religion or philosophy could either. Somehow, I clung to the notion that beneath it all there was a truth that could stand the test of my honest questions.

Setting aside the stylistic and cultural differences I had with the church, I began a search for the truth. I started reading books that would help me find the places where faith and reason intersect. Great thinkers like Aristotle, who talked about how there is much more to reality than science could explain, referred to these issues (the realities that lay beyond the physical sciences) as *meta*physical. Augustine asserted that our souls would be restless until they found their rest in God. Pascal wrote about a God-shaped vacuum inside each of us, a void that only God could fill. These and numbers of other great thinkers helped me come to the conclusion that we are not alone in an impersonal universe and we are not the random result of a cosmic accident.

Because the real meaning of life goes beyond what can be analyzed under a microscope or programmed onto a computer chip, explaining the *how* of life just wasn't enough for me. I longed to know the *why* of life. Real meaning in life is more than amusement, more than self-expression, more than defining, systematizing, and reorganizing all the data we could ever collect. Such things will never answer the cry of our souls because we all are looking for something way beyond ourselves. I believe that something is a Someone.

Christianity teaches that the infinite, personal God has clearly revealed Himself. The testimonies of curiosity, awareness, nature, cause and effect, and conscience offer a *general* revelation of God. The Christian faith offers *specific* revelation of God from two sources: the written word of the Bible and the living word of Jesus Christ. They both shed light on the nature of God.

Through the Bible we can know about God. But more importantly, we discover that we can also actually *know* God. Jesus Christ, God the Son, entered time and history to make a way for us to have a relationship with our Creator. He came to invite us to become members of an invisible kingdom, a spiritual kingdom, one that is not limited to the physical realm. It's through Christ that we can find real significance in life. It's through Him that we are offered God's forgiveness and mercy, and it is by His love that we can find our way back home to our Father's house.

- *The world is full of books about religion, what's so unique about the Bible?*

- *How does a book as old as the Bible relate to us today?*

- *Isn't the Bible full of contradictions?*

- *In a nutshell, what is the Bible really all about?*

- *Who wrote the Bible and when was it written?*

- *Why are there so many translations of the Bible?*

- *Why do I have so much trouble understanding the Bible?*

5

How Do We Know the Bible Is God's Word?

All the wisdom of this world is but a tiny raft upon which we must set sail when we leave this earth. If only there was a firmer foundation upon which to sail, perhaps some divine word.

—*Socrates*

Yearbooks

The other day I happened upon my old high school yearbook (I know what you're thinking, but don't worry. I won't be launching into a melodramatic retelling of my good ol' glory days). As I leafed through its pages, I was struck by the fact that something as simple as a yearbook could evoke such vivid memories. There were photos of events like football games, Homecoming, the Prom, and Graduation Day. There were snapshot reminders of relationships with my best buddies, of girls I wished I had had the guts to ask out but never did, and of teachers who poured their hearts out trying to get me to pay attention long enough to learn the difference between a noun and a verb. There were tokens and mementos of clubs and cliques, athletics and academics. The yearbook was an overview of the people, places, and events that sum up those four years I spent at Falls Church High School in northern Virginia.

In a much more significant way, the Bible is a similar kind of book. It tells us about the people, places, and events that have been a part of the human drama for centuries. While it doesn't contain any photographs, the Bible does paint fairly detailed portraits of real men and women from all walks of life and how they related to each other and to God.

But unlike most high school yearbooks that end up filled with those sappy, unrealistic "you're really sweet, cute, and nice...don't ever change" inscriptions, the Bible tells us the honest truth about ourselves. It speaks about how we have all gone our own selfish ways and how much we need the grace and forgiveness of God in our lives. And when the Bible calls for us to change, it even tells us how that change can take place—that God Himself will be the one to change us if we are just willing.

Most importantly, as we read the pages of the Bible, it tells us about God. It reveals who God is, what God is like, what He wants from us, and how we can come to know Him. It is a love story about God's relentless pursuit of those who would yield their lives to Him.

The Criticism

Of course, the Bible has its detractors, but isn't it ironic that many of the people who denounce the Bible most passionately have never actually read it? What are they basing their criticism on? Others struggle with the idea that it is the source of divine revelation. While many of these people would say they believe in God, one wonders what kind of God they believe in. Is their God mute? Is He unable to speak? Is their God not intelligent enough to employ at least some basic communication skills to convey a message to us?

One thing the Bible demonstrates very clearly is that God is not mute. The God of the Bible has spoken. He has employed several means to communicate with humanity: direct, verbal communication, carvings on stone tablets, the words of prophets and priests, angelic messengers, and thundering clouds. The God of the Bible is so intent on being heard that one time He even opened the mouth of a donkey to get the attention of a thick-headed prophet. And after trying for years to get a hearing from humanity via these means, God finally decided to leave the comforts of heaven, put on some human skin, and come to speak directly with as many as would hear Him. Perhaps the communication problem is not from God's side of things!

Isn't this what it all comes down to: If God were to speak, would we be willing to hear? If you believe that God is really there, that He created the heavens and the earth and is the designer of the human eye, the juggler of stars, and the painter of sunsets, why on earth would you think God couldn't speak? If God can draft DNA, why wouldn't He be able to inspire some of His people to write down what He wanted us to know? Believing the Bible is not nearly so preposterous as believing that God exists but is somehow unable or unwilling to communicate with us.

So let's ask the basic questions: What *is* the Bible? When was it written and by whom? How can such an ancient book be relevant to us today?

The Details

The Bible is a compilation of 66 books, divided into two major sections—the Old Testament and the New Testament. The word *testament* is another word for a promise, a pledge, or a covenant, and both parts of the Bible detail the covenants God has made with His people.

The writings of the Bible were composed over a period of approximately 1400 years (roughly 1300 B.C. to A.D. 100) and were originally written in three different languages—Hebrew, Aramaic (a hybrid language similar to Hebrew and spoken throughout the Near East from c. 300 B.C to c. A.D. 650), and ancient Greek. The writers of the various books came from every kind of socioeconomic background including peasants, prophets, kings, fishermen, doctors, poets, accountants, and statesmen. They included royalty and common folk, rich and poor, educated and uneducated alike. Perhaps that's one of the reasons why so many millions of people have been able to find something in the Bible that relates to their own situation in life.

The Amazing Unity of the Bible

I don't know if you've ever noticed how hard it is to order pizza when you're with a group of people, even if they're people you know well and get along with. The larger the group, the more difficult the process becomes. Two people like veggie only, two like the butcher shop's variety of meats. Three people want thick crust, one wants thin, another wants extra-extra-extra cheese. Getting even ten people to agree on what kind of pizza to order can be downright impossible.

That's also the way it can be with thoughts and ideas about religion. There are even more ideas about God, faith, and spirituality than there are topping combinations for pizza. Finding any agreement on what is true about God and what He has communicated to us can seem impossible. But this demonstrates one of the unique truths about the Bible. It wasn't written by some sort of mountain-dwelling, navel-gazing guru who ate hallucinogenic mushrooms one night and had a wild dream about what God is like. Instead it was written by a diverse group of individuals who represent a broad cross section of humanity. And God didn't override the identities of the people

He inspired to write these books. The personality of each writer comes through loud and clear, each exhibiting a unique style.

In short, the Bible doesn't reflect just one single person's experience with the God of the universe. It's the result of God inspiring over 40 different individuals to write down the things He wanted us to know. And in spite of its wide variety of authors and their diverse backgrounds, there's an amazing harmony and unity in the Bible. The unified message of the Bible is the story of God's plan of redemption. Each author and every book paints some part of the mural. It's as if 40 different people got inspired one night and could actually order pizza together!

The Uniqueness of the Bible

The Bible is a truly unique book. No other book in history has been translated into more languages or distributed more widely around the world. World leaders invoke its wisdom, philosophers praise its truth, and countless millions have benefited from the hope and comfort found in its pages. The Bible contains a message that rings true in the hearts of hungry souls.

Down through the centuries the Bible has inspired such notables as Isaac Newton, who declared the Scriptures to be the most exalted philosophy. George Washington, the first president of the United States, said, "It is impossible to govern the world without God and the Bible." Philosopher Immanuel Kant wrote that "a single line in the Bible has consoled me more than all the books I have ever read." And Theodore Roosevelt once said, "A thorough knowledge of the Bible is worth more than a college education."

Yet in spite of all it has to offer, for many people the Bible remains unopened, unapproachable, and nothing more than a graduation gift or a place to record the family tree. Why is this so? There may be several answers, but like any other book, the Bible must be read before it can be fully appreciated.

The Relevance

As you read through the Bible, you'll soon discover that its message is timeless. Although people back in Bible times didn't drive cars, talk on cellular phones, or surf the Web, they did share in common a lot of the same human experiences you and I have today. They wrestled with real-life problems such as broken relationships, greed, doubt, fear, depression, anger, disease, and financial troubles. Just like us, they had a deep-seated need for significance and security. They wanted to love and be loved by God, their friends, and their families. The common characteristic we share with them is that none of us can face those problems successfully on our own. We all need God's help.

The Honest Truth About Ourselves

One of the benefits we get from reading the Bible is that it provides an honest look at ourselves. All the characters of the Bible are presented candidly and honestly, just as they really were. Even the great King David, a central and heroic figure in the Old Testament referred to as "a man after God's own heart," is shown as someone who was tempted to lust, didn't have the moral strength to resist, and acted on his lust by committing adultery with another man's wife. He then sent the woman's husband off to the frontlines of a fierce battle, thus ensuring this man's death so he could take the man's wife as his own. In the writing of the Bible, there was no political spin machine enlisted to make us think David had not sinned. We are shown what he did, told that it was wrong, and even shown what the consequences of his actions were (see 2 Samuel chapters 11 and 12).

So one thing is very clear: You can be sure the Bible will give you an honest look at the human condition. It reveals the good, the bad, and the ugly. And that's one of the reasons the Bible rings true for so many people; it corresponds to reality by being honest about the weaknesses of some of history's most influential figures.

The Authority of the Bible

Socrates once said: "All the wisdom of this world is but a tiny raft upon which we must set sail when we leave this earth. If only there was a firmer foundation upon which to sail, perhaps some divine word."

Without a doubt, Socrates had one of the sharpest minds of any person who ever lived. Yet even Socrates recognized the limitations of human wisdom. He acknowledged that in our search for real meaning in this life and hope for what happens to us in the next, we would have to find another source of truth. And Socrates knew this kind of wisdom could not and would not ever be of human origin, not ultimately authored in the mind or heart of any man or woman. It would have to come from a source higher than humanity and be what he called a "divine word."

That is precisely what the Bible claims to be: a divine word, the Word of God. That is why it has earned such a place of authority in the lives of so many people. Through the ministry of the Holy Spirit, the Word of God becomes a lamp unto our feet and a light unto our path. It illuminates the ground beneath our feet (as a metaphor for our current situation in life), and it also illuminates the path ahead to give us direction for the future.

The Questions

Socrates liked to stir people up. He was known to ask his students some pretty tough questions to challenge them in their thinking. It was his hope that they would discover truth without him having to spoon-feed it to them.

Among all the known species, we human beings are unique in our intelligence and in our capacity to think and reason. Not many cockroaches, camels, or codfish seem concerned with questions about the origin of the universe, the meaning of life, or thoughts about the existence of God. This doesn't mean that other species are without intelligence or skills. We see amazing engineering skills when we watch a spider spin her web, and we may learn something about aerodynamics by studying the flight of an eagle. However, no other creature ponders subjects like truth, meaning, morality, and destiny. These issues are simply beyond mere animal instinct.

Down through the centuries, philosophers and religious thinkers have dealt with "the big questions" in a variety of different ways. There have been those who, believing in the power of human reason, have argued that mankind would someday be able to come up with satisfying answers to any question that might be posed. But so far that has not happened.

Other thinkers have denied the importance of these questions. They have set the questions aside, declaring that since we can never *really know* about these things, any attempt to do so would be vain speculation and a waste of our time. But both of these ways of dealing with our questions leave out another viable possibility.

Recognizing the limitations of human reason and conceding that there are many things beyond the reach of our intelligence, many have acknowledged the necessity of looking outside ourselves for answers to these ultimate questions. One of the greatest minds of the seventeenth century, mathematician and philosopher Blaise Pascal, concluded: "Reason's last step is the recognition that there are an infinite number of things which are beyond it. It is merely feeble if it does not go as far as to realize that."

Let's face it. In spite of all our incredible scientific, technological, and philosophical accomplishments, human reason simply hasn't been able to offer satisfying answers to these ultimate questions of life. If we are to find the answers to our deepest questions, we will need to search outside ourselves. So, where should we turn?

The Revelation

John Henry Newman once said: "As prayer is the voice of man to God, so revelation is the voice of God to man." Revelation is a term derived from the Latin *revelare* meaning "to unveil." Revelation provides knowledge that is otherwise unavailable to us, knowledge that we could not access by thinking harder or investigating more. Revelation offers us knowledge that is simply beyond our reach, beyond human discovery. Through revelation, information is disclosed to us by an outside, more informed source.

Let me try to express this another way. While the Bible deals with revelation on a divine-to-human level, a simple, human-to-human example of revelation would be a parent who tells a young child that the moon's light is not its own, but that it is a reflection of the sun's light. The child could not have figured this truth out for himself. It is simply beyond the child's reach. But as they grow, children learn many new things from the credible "revelations" of their moms and dads, older brothers and sisters, friends or teachers. Even though all the subtle nuances of every answer may not be fully understood, these revelations are the truth made available in a simple enough form to be understood. So it is with God's revelation to us. In the pages of the Bible He tells us truths that we couldn't discover for ourselves.

The Means

Just because the Bible (or any other source) *claims* to offer divine revelation does not mean that it does. Since we are reasoning creatures, we cannot blindly accept just any revelation that claims to be of divine origin without testing its veracity. This raises a question. If God were to reveal things about Himself to us, what means would He use to do it? How would the messages be conveyed?

It seems to me that true divine revelation would need to have at least three characteristics. First, it would have to be offered in an intelligible language that humans could understand, write down, study, analyze, translate, and preserve for others to consider. If it were God's intention to communicate to as many people as possible, it seems unlikely He would offer revelation in a secret language that could only be understood by a spiritually gifted prophet or an elite few. Rather, God would likely choose a commonly used language. Such is the case with the Bible.

Second, divine revelation would be informative. It would contain propositional truth about God, mankind, morality, and the universe. Its statements would give these subjects definition and show how they relate to each other. And while information about the infinite God could never be exhaustive, that does not mean it can't be accurate. What is revealed would be specific and applicable to real, everyday life. Such is the case with the Bible.

Third, whenever divine revelation speaks about issues we already know something about (for example, science or history) it would be relatively accurate to what we have come to know. When the Bible speaks historically, we should not find historical evidence that clearly and conclusively contradicts what the Bible says. When the Bible speaks about science, it should not contradict what has been proven beyond a shadow of doubt by scientific research. Also, when the Bible makes statements about human beings and their nature, those statements should generally hold up to what we can see in the mirror or in people on the street. For example, if the Bible were to claim that humans can live underwater or that trees can talk (not in a poetic sense but literally), it would be fair to discount the Bible as a source of revelation. Divine revelation should be true to the realities which have been conclusively confirmed. Once again, such is the case with the Bible.

Finally, while a credible source of divine revelation might unveil knowledge that is *beyond* reason, it must not contradict the fundamentals of sound reason, otherwise we would not be able to come to a firm belief regarding the truth it claims. The Law of Non-Contradiction, the Law of Cause and Effect, and the basic reliability of sense perception should still be in play. Christianity is rational, but it is not mere rationalism. It is reasonable but it does not depend solely on human reason. As Mortimer Adler has said: "My chief reason for choosing Christianity was because the mysteries were incomprehensible. What's the point of revelation if we could figure it out ourselves? If it were wholly comprehensible, then it would be just another philosophy."

I find it quite satisfying that the Christian faith has both verities and mysteries in it, that it is full of things we can verify by reason, and it contains other things that leave us standing in wide-eyed wonder. Reason gives us confidence; revelation gives us hope. The Bible speaks to us with both.

The Accuracy of the Bible

Some have questioned the credibility of the Bible because of its age and the number of times it has been translated. But the Bible (and specifically, the New Testament) is perhaps the most credible of ancient texts in existence. The New Testament was completed almost entirely within the first century A.D., close to the time Christ walked the earth, and was written by people who either knew Jesus personally or were close to someone who did.

All 27 books of the New Testament were written between A.D. 45 and A.D. 90. Someone may complain saying, "That's a pretty long time between when Jesus lived and when these things were written. How can we possibly believe the New Testament record is accurate? As many times as it was copied and recopied, it would surely have lost some of its accuracy, wouldn't it?" These are fair questions, so let's take a moment to judge the credibility of the New Testament the same way we would any other ancient text.

I think there are three things which are important to consider: 1. When was the ancient text originally written? 2. How many manuscript copies exist? and 3. How big a gap is there between when the original text was written and the dates of the earliest surviving manuscript copies?

For instance, scholars tell us that Homer's *Iliad* was originally written around 900 B.C. There are 643 manuscript copies in existence, the earliest being dated at 400 B.C. That's a 500-year gap. Or take Caesar's *Gallic Wars*, written 58–50 B.C., with only 10 manuscript copies in existence, and the earliest copy dated at A.D. 900. That's almost a 1,000-year gap. Even worse, how about Plato's *Tetralogies,* dated 427–347 B.C. There are only 7 manuscripts in existence, with the earliest copy dated at A.D. 900. That's a 1,200-year gap.

So how does the New Testament compare to these other ancient texts? As I mentioned above, all 27 books of the New Testament were completed by the end of the first century A.D. There are 5,366 manuscripts or partial manuscripts of the New Testament in existence, and the earliest manuscript copies have been dated to within 100 years of their original composition. That's less than a 100-year gap![4]

If you judge the New Testament the same way you do other ancient texts, the New Testament is clearly the most trustworthy of all ancient documents. In the writings of the New Testament we have a very credible source of historical data.

The Contradictions?

One of the most common criticisms aimed at the Bible is this: "Isn't the Bible full of contradictions?" Now, "full" is a pretty strong word. One gets the image of a book with blatant contradictions on every page and in every paragraph. Once again, this complaint is usually put forward by people who have never

actually read the Bible. If asked to point out one of these contradictions, they usually shrug their shoulders and confess that
they don't have any specific examples.

Of course there are difficulties in translation and interpreta-
tion, but these are not about issues which, even if proved true,
would disprove the overall message of the Bible. We would be
foolish to discount the Bible based on a few insignificant trivi-
alities.

There are certainly things in the Bible that could be classified
as *paradox*, that is, something which appears to be a contradiction but may very well be true. But a paradox is not a contradiction. Most apparent contradictions in the Bible are pretty
easily resolved by taking a look at some additional historical or
cultural information. Others can be resolved by allowing for lit-
erary genre, such as when the writer/speaker employs parable
metaphor, or poetry. Another thing that is often mistaken as a
contradiction is *mystery*, and the Bible contains some incredible
mysteries. A mystery can be defined as something unexplainable
but not inconceivable; truths made known by divine revelation
and believed through faith would certainly qualify as mysteries.

The Translations

I am often asked, "Why are there so many different translations
of the Bible?" Granted, there are quite a few. But clearly the Bible
itself is not the reason for this. The simple fact is that the English language is quite fluid and is continually evolving. Words
come to have different meanings with each cultural shift.
Because of this fact, if we are to understand what the Bible
writers meant at their time, in their particular cultural setting,
we will constantly be adjusting our translations of the ancient
texts to reflect the authors' originally intended meaning.

(If you have had difficulty reading the Bible because of some
language barrier, let me encourage you to look around for
another translation. There are many available and there is sure

to be one that will speak in terms you can understand. Most Christian booksellers will be able to offer you helpful advice in picking one out.)

So What's in the Bible?

In the end, it is the content of the Bible that provides us with the most convincing proof of its truthfulness and authority. I have often used the acronym E.A.T.E.A. (pronounced E.T.) to describe how the Bible unveils divine knowledge in these fundamental categories of thought: Epistemology, Anthropology, Theology, Ethics, and Aesthetics.

The Bible Speaks About Epistemology

The fear of the Lord is the beginning of knowledge; fools despise wisdom and instruction (Proverbs 1:7).

Epistemology is the study of the nature, sources, and limits of knowledge. It seeks to answer the questions of what we can know and how it can be known. There are many opinions about precisely what we can know and with how much certainty we can know it. But somewhere, after all the arguments have been heard, we all have to put our intellectual feet down on something as a starting place.

The Bible distinguishes between the "wisdom of this world" (1 Corinthians 2:4-7) and the "wisdom of God" (1 Corinthians 2:7-14). The wisdom of this world is limited to what man can know on his own without the help of God through revelation. It is limited to knowledge we can obtain through our five senses. If someone holds to a belief that God does not exist and that the natural world is all there is, then obviously, matters of spirituality will not make sense to that person.

The Bible teaches that human nature includes a spiritual component and that our five senses are ineffective in comprehending the spiritual realm (1 Corinthians 2:14). Through reading and hearing the truth of the Bible, the Spirit of God brings faith to our hearts by revealing the mysteries of God to us and offering insights into who we are as spiritual and moral creatures.

The Bible acknowledges that humans are intelligent (Isaiah 1:18), but that real knowing begins with a fear and respect of God, the author of knowledge (Proverbs 1:7). Wisdom, the ability to efficiently employ knowledge, is also to be found in the fear and respect of God (Proverbs 9:10). The Bible claims to be God's timeless word to mankind (Isaiah 40:8; Mark 13:31). As such, it offers us access to an incredible wealth of knowledge (2 Timothy 3:16-17). The Bible is indeed a divine word, illuminating all of life, offering hope for the future and providing that "firmer foundation on which to sail" for which Socrates longed.

But as gatekeepers of our own minds, we must recognize that the wisdom of the Bible is not preprogrammed into us. We have to take the time to read it ourselves and to meditate on it, becoming ever more familiar with the truth it contains. The Bible is a means of grace, the hearing of which gives rise to faith in our hearts. As we search the depths of the Scripture, a practical working knowledge of the things of God is revealed to us by the Spirit of God.

The Bible Speaks About Anthropology

And God created man in His own image, in the image of God He created him; male and female He created them. And God blessed them; and God said to them, "Be fruitful and multiply, and fill the earth, and subdue it; and rule over the fish of the sea and over the birds of the sky, and over every living thing that moves on the earth" (Genesis 1:27-28).

Anthropology is the study of the human person. From the Bible's pages we find helpful information about our origin, purpose, and destiny, as well as honest information about our nature and character.

First, the Bible speaks about our origin—that we were lovingly and carefully designed by God (Psalm 139:13-16). This stands in contrast to the atheistic, antisupernatural view, which suggests we are the result of an accidental arrangement of chemicals. The Bible's view leads us to hope. The other view ultimately leads us to despair.

Second, the Bible speaks about our purpose. It tells us that among all things created, humans are the only part of creation that was made *imago dei*, in God's image and likeness. On that basis, we may deduce that human beings were created to reflect the image of God. Since God is infinite, every finite human life has value, dignity, and purpose because each of us can reflect God's image. You might say humanity is like a giant disco mirror ball, each of us one of the small mirror panels reflecting some small part of the infinite God.

In the Bible's view, our destiny is to be restored to our function as image bearers of God by coming to know Him personally, loving Him fully, and living with Him forever. The Bible also teaches that each of us will remain a unique individual personality throughout eternity. This stands in contrast to other religions that view God as an impersonal force and each human a part of that force, destined upon death to be assimilated into the impersonal, cosmic unity.

The Bible Speaks About Theology

In the beginning God...(Genesis 1:1).

Theology is the study of God, His nature, and His relationship with mankind. Without the revelation of the Bible, we would know very little about God, and what we could know would be vague at best. But the Bible offers an answer to the question "Does God exist?" by pointing out that before anything else existed, God already was, and that He created everything *ex nihilo*, or out of nothing (Genesis 1:1).

In answer to the question "What is God like?" the Bible gives us many insights into His character: God is love (1 John 4:8); God will one day be our judge (Romans 2:5); God is forgiving to those who confess their sin and repent (1 John 1:9); God knows everything (Psalm 139:1-6); God is supreme and almighty (1 Chronicles 29:11). And above all, the Bible reveals that God is personal and wants us to know Him.

The Bible also documents God's actions in history. This does not mean the Bible documents *all* of God's actions on this planet or elsewhere in the universe. But we are given exactly the information God wants us to know (Revelation 22:18-19). That is to say, as God inspired the writing and directed the compilation of the Bible, He did it with intention, purpose, and design. The information in the Bible was not accidentally discovered by us nor was it accidentally revealed (2 Timothy 3:14-17). God is behind both the revealing and the understanding of His Word.

The Bible is a book about restoring the relationship between an almighty God and the creatures He created (1 Corinthians 1:21). It's about a relationship between a loving Father and His often wayward children (Galatians 4:4-6). It talks about our rebellion and God's forgiveness, how in spite of our self-centeredness, there is a way we can have peace with God through Christ. It's about the God who is there and His eternal plan for humanity.

The Bible Speaks About Ethics

For such is the will of God that by doing right you may silence the ignorance of foolish men (1 Peter 2:15).

Ethics are the set of moral principles and values by which we determine right and wrong. Everyone has a general sense of the moral law. Everyone understands that there are some things that are "right" and some that are "wrong" in life. We have all found ourselves saying, "Hey, that's unfair!" and if there is such a thing as "fair," then there has to be some standard, a moral law by which we can judge what is fair and what is unfair. Where did this law come from? Since it is propositional, not biological, moral law must have an intelligence behind it. Then who is the moral lawgiver?

The Bible teaches that there is a nonhuman, nonrelative basis and source of universal moral law. Contemporary theologian John Stott has said:

> Christians cannot go along with secularists when they agitate for unlimited permissiveness in social and ethical terms, nor when they foolishly imagine that "free thought" is intellectual freedom or that "free sex" is moral freedom. For Christians are convinced that neither truth nor righteousness is relative, since God has given us (by revelation) absolute standards both of what is true and of what is right.[5]

We live in an era when there is great confusion about issues of public and private morality, and many people now believe that moral values are relative or "up to the individual." This confusion arises in part from the fact that we are a pluralistic society. There is disagreement on which set of values should serve as the norm for all of society.

The only remedy for a culture or an individual is to recognize that we need an outside source, one that offers clarity on what is right and what is wrong, a source that we can use like a compass to help us find our way.

The Bible Speaks About Aesthetics

For since the creation of the world His invisible attributes, His eternal power and divine nature, have been clearly seen, being understood through what has been made, so that they are without excuse (Romans 1:20).

Aesthetics is the branch of philosophy which deals with the nature and appreciation of beauty and art. The Bible tells us that throughout the created universe we see evidence of God's creativity and His penchant for beauty. In Genesis, the Bible says that after God created the elements of the physical universe, there was no form, and that all was in chaos. Then God began to design and arrange, to bring order and form to the cosmos. He created light, land, vegetation, and all living things. The book of Genesis tells us that God stopped and assessed His work and saw that it was "good."

In the Scriptures, beauty has a purpose. It points like a road sign to the Author of beauty. The significance of the beauty of nature declares God's glory, reminding us of God's majesty, power, authority, and generosity. God did not have to make anything, as He was not lacking in any way. He did not need to make humanity because He was lonely or needed someone to talk to. God simply chose to create as an expression of His own creativity and was generous enough to give humanity the ability to appreciate all He has made. That's why we stand in silent awe beside the mighty ocean, dumbfounded at the foot of the majestic mountains, or drawn heavenward under a star-filled sky. There is unmatched beauty all around us, and all of creation cries, "Glory to God!"

God Has Spoken

God's divine revelation in the Bible speaks to both the heart and the mind. If the Bible only spoke to the heart, it would leave us open to all sorts of romantic delusions. If it only spoke to the mind, it would leave us with a lifeless and hollow intellectualism. How wise of God to intentionally reach out to us in this holistic way.

In Psalm 32:8-9, God spoke through King David and said this:

> I will instruct you and teach you in the way which you should go; I will counsel you with My eye upon you. Do not be as the horse or as the mule which have no understanding, whose trappings include bit and bridle

to hold them in check, otherwise they will not come near to you.

God's guidance does not come under compulsion as in the way we guide a horse or mule through the use of bit and bridle. Rather, He will guide us with instruction and counsel so that we can employ the God-given gifts of intelligence, reason, understanding, and free will. He will use His Word, the Bible, to teach us about Himself, about how we can know Him, and how we should conduct our lives on earth with each other. But God does not force this information on us. We will have to open the book and read it, meditate on it, ponder what it says, and pray for insight to learn what it means. So, when you read the Bible, use the eyes of both your mind and your heart. Pray for the Holy Spirit to teach you. Ask God to show you what you need to see, and then ask Him for the courage and will to respond to what He shows you to do.

- *The world has seen many great religious leaders, so what's so special about Jesus?*

- *Why has Jesus Christ remained such an important figure in human history?*

- *How do we know what Jesus was really like?*

- *What makes people think that Jesus was the Son of God?*

- *Why did Jesus have to die on the cross?*

- *Everybody quotes and misquotes Jesus all the time. What is the essence of His teachings?*

- *He lived so long ago—how do the teachings of Christ relate to me today?*

6

What's So Special About Jesus?

And coming to His hometown He began teaching them in their synagogue, so that they became astonished, and said, "Where did this man get this wisdom, and these miraculous powers?"

—*Matthew 13:54*

Souvenir Shops

Nashville became our hometown in the mid 1980s. During that time, the popularity of country music was on the rise. Country music celebrities knew they had made it to the big time when they could afford to open their own souvenir shops on the north end of the famed Music Row. This shopping district became known as Souvenir Row. It was a beehive of activity for fans and tourists. At any one of these shops you could buy CDs, cassettes, posters, and photo magazines of popular country music stars, as well as coffee cups, cowboy hats, T-shirts, and beach towels. Some shops even had "cars of the stars" on display. There were lots of flashing lights, free food, and karaoke music performed by sequined, would-be country stars. All this glitz was designed to pull in as many fans and tourists as possible.

If you had come for a visit, were short on time, and were still trying to figure out which was the *best* souvenir shop (you know, the one where you could find that special Elvis Hair Shampoo & Conditioner you'd been looking for), it could get confusing. Which shop should you go to? More than one had a sign that boasted "The Biggest Selection!" or "Best Souvenir Shop in Nashville!" As the shopaholic's lament goes, "So many shops, so little time."

When it comes to religious leaders, it's a little like those Nashville souvenir shops. So many have been called "special" in one way or another. And a handful of them have stood the test of time, exerting a lasting impact on succeeding generations. Some of these historic figures have led their followers to higher understandings of issues like peace, justice, social equality, and compassion for those less fortunate. Others have motivated their followers to pursue lives of self-denial, simplicity, and solitude. And still others have enlightened us by teaching with great insight about God, humanity, and the universe we all live in.

But among all these great religious leaders, there is one who stands out from the crowd. His impact has been greater than any other religious figure in history. Oddly enough, He never made a big deal out of social or political issues. He didn't appear to be concerned about image or celebrity. As a matter of fact, He often avoided crowds. He never appeared on television, never had a radio talk show, and never built a mega-church. He never went to seminary, never wore a suit and tie, and never carried a King James Bible. He never sang *Rock of Ages, Amazing Grace, Kum-Bah-Yah,* or *Pass It On*. And I'd venture to say that if He had lived in Nashville in the mid 1980s, He probably wouldn't have had the kind of celebrity that would have justified opening a souvenir shop on Music Row.

His name was Jesus of Nazareth, and He was a poor Jewish carpenter who walked the planet for a little over 30 years in first century Palestine.

The Real Jesus of History

I'm aware that you probably already have an image in your mind when you read the name "Jesus Christ." Perhaps it's a nice image attached to a Sunday school workbook you drew pictures in as a child. Or maybe it's a negative image created by something you heard one of His clumsy followers say when talking to you about salvation as you sat together on an airplane. Or maybe your image of Jesus is vague and confused, scrambled by a series of hard questions that plague your heart and mind.

Whatever the case, in the next few pages I'd like to invite you to take a fresh look at Jesus. Why don't you push the reset button in your heart and mind, setting aside your preconceived ideas, so you can approach the real Jesus of history without any baggage.

The first thing we need to clear up is that Jesus of Nazareth, the one called the Christ, was not a folk hero or a mythological figure like Jack in the Beanstalk or Zeus. Jesus was an actual human being, a real person, with hair, eyes, a nose, a chin, knuckles, knees, and toes. Had you lived back then, you could have touched Him on the shoulder, looked Him in the eye, and felt Him pat you on the back. You could have seen Him smile at the approach of children and heard Him speak as He taught the Sermon on the Mount.

What do we know about His life? Well, as the Christmas song tells us, He was born in the "little town of Bethlehem" a few miles south of Jerusalem. His family moved north to the Galilean town of Nazareth where He grew up learning the trade of carpentry from His legal father, Joseph. As far as we know, Jesus worked in the family business until He was 30 years of age, most likely building tables, chairs, doors, plows, and oxen yokes for His neighbors in and around Nazareth. Given what we know about Him now, it's safe to assume that as a carpenter, Jesus probably did some fairly creative work. I wouldn't be surprised at all if He and Joseph had hung a sign in the window of their shop that read "Best Carpentry Shop in Nazareth."

A Case of Unlikely Celebrity

Nonetheless, before He started His public ministry Jesus probably would not have been the first person you thought of when casting your vote for *The Jerusalem Journal's* "Man of the Year" award. He was poor and lived in an occupied territory. During His public ministry He was disliked by the religious establishment, and at the end of His ministry even the crowds who followed Him turned against Him. Then He was hung on a Roman cross to die the death of a common criminal convicted on a trumped-up charge brought against Him.

And yet, in the 2,000 years since Jesus walked the earth, more has been written about Him than any other figure in human history—more than Julius Caesar, King Arthur, Elvis, and John Kennedy all put together. The teachings have been studied, scrutinized, and analyzed by more people than the teachings of Aristotle, Albert Einstein, and Sigmund Freud combined. The simple truth is this: Jesus of Nazareth is the most talked about individual who ever lived.

A Case of Mistaken Identity

To find the real Jesus, we must look past all the popular misconceptions about who He is. It shouldn't surprise us that someone who has been the subject of so much discussion is misrepresented from time to time. This is certainly the case with Jesus. Some have reduced Jesus to a hippie-like, guru philosopher whose only message is peace, love, and forgiveness. Others portray Jesus as a harsh and angry prophet, bent on executing judgment and meting out punishment for even the slightest moral failure or social faux pas. Still others have depicted Jesus as a bisexual or a homosexual, as if sexuality was the central issue by which Jesus defined Himself.

So who was the real Jesus? Was He like the common pictures of a good-looking, long-haired, West Coast "surfer dude" with deep-blue eyes, a sharp jawline, and a dark tan? Or could He be like the flannelgraph Sunday school materials portray Him—a peaceful looking teacher clothed in robe and sandals? In these pictures He's almost always smiling and holding a lamb or a child in His arms. That's nice.

But how does that fit with the Jesus who turns over tables in the Temple and then throws everyone out? And what's this about Him excoriating the religious leaders of His day for their legalism and hypocrisy? Why did He raise moral standards to such unreachable heights? Did he demand perfection from those who would follow Him?

When you compare them with the best historical accounts of Jesus, most of these modern ideas about Jesus can be seen as nothing more than fanciful, revisionist interpretations. They have little connection with the historical facts. They reveal a tendency to treat Jesus' life and teachings like you would a salad bar, picking the items you like and leaving the rest. Worse still, some people have brought their own ingredients to the salad bar and left them there, hoping others will try Jesus *their* way.

There are a lot of people who form their concept of the real Jesus from these imaginative misrepresentations. They come to believe that Jesus was really the equivalent of the way some actor in a film has portrayed Him, the way He looks in a painting or on a poster, or the way an author arbitrarily describes Him in a book. But these ideas about Jesus are usually just the musings of irrational romantics who use Jesus like a religious action figure, dressing Him up in the costume of their choice: one time as a mysterious, transcendental guru; the next as a humanistic, super-social worker; and the next as a single-issue political activist.

Where should we look to find the real Jesus? As with any pursuit of historical fact, we should search for sources which display the qualities we associate with credible historical evidence. These would be sources that will give us specific details from eyewitnesses that contain verifiable names, events, places, and dates, information that can be corroborated by outside sources that have themselves proven to be credible. From this kind of material it would be possible to get an idea of who the real Jesus of history was, what He actually did, and what He really taught.

The Biography of Christ

To use an old adage, I suggest we get it "straight from the horse's mouth." We should look at who Jesus claimed to be. The essence of His personal claims will tell us more about Him than anything else. They will reveal why He was so different and why His message to humanity was so convincing, so convicting, and so timeless.

Now, there is one small difficulty we face in getting the "straight scoop." Jesus did not leave any writings behind. He never wrote a book Himself. But then again, neither did Socrates. Yet we have learned much about Socrates and what he said through the writings of one of his students, a man named Plato.

The writing of a good biographer can be a window into someone's life, especially if that person were an eyewitness to the key events of the story. If you were no longer around and I wanted to know something about you, but you had left no tangible record of yourself—no photos, no book, no videotape or voice recordings—I would not be left in the dark. The best thing I could do would be to look to the people who knew you and were closest to you. If they told me about you, then I would know something of what you were really like and the kinds of things you said and did. And even though some might not have the whole story, by checking and crosschecking my sources I could still get a pretty credible account about the real you.

That's exactly what we find in reading the New Testament. It contains four personal and intimate biographies of Jesus written by eyewitnesses who were His students and friends. It's like looking at a scrapbook about Jesus' life. The first four books of the New Testament—Matthew, Mark, Luke, and John—give us a record of His birth, life, teachings, deeds, death, resurrection, and ascension.

Two of these books, Matthew and John, were written by men who were actual disciples of Jesus. That is to say, they knew Him personally. They walked Palestinian roads together, sat around campfires together, stayed up late at night telling stories and laughing until they all cried. They heard the very words of Jesus as He preached powerful sermons in synagogues, on hillsides, at the shorelines, or in the cities. They saw with their own eyes as Jesus opened the eyes of the blind and the ears of the deaf. They helped Jesus pass out the food that day He fed thousands from a little boy's lunch pail, and they witnessed other miracles from His hand.

Mark's Gospel, though actually written down by Mark, is believed to have been taken from an account verbally dictated by Peter, one of Jesus' closest disciples and friends. Through Mark, Peter gives us his version of the amazing deeds of the real Jesus of history. Peter was there in that overcrowded house on the day Jesus commanded a severely paralyzed man to take up his stretcher and walk. He was in the room when Jesus commanded a little dead girl to come back to life and watched her rise up. He was in that nearly swamped boat when Jesus commanded a violent storm to be still, and it stopped immediately. And on one unique occasion, Peter, James, and John were up on a mountaintop with Jesus when they got to peek behind the curtain of heaven as Jesus straddled the natural world and the supernatural world right before their very eyes. They got to eavesdrop as Jesus talked with none other than the Old Testament heroes Moses and Elijah.

Luke was an educated physician. With a doctor's eye for details, he tries to provide the most accurate portrait possible, telling us about the real Jesus of history. In his opening remarks he describes the arduous process of "having *investigated everything carefully* from the beginning" and then tells us the purpose of his writing, which was "so that you might *know the exact truth* about the things you have been taught." Sounds like a man who was out to find out what really happened and report with precision the facts he uncovered. Isn't it interesting that a man of science would become one of the key persons to investigate and convey the truth about the most significant religious figure in history?

Luke is believed to have written his record of the life and teachings of Christ with the help of Mary, the mother of Jesus. Knowing what my mom knows about me, I think Mary could have provided some fairly credible eyewitness accounts of the real Jesus of history. Wouldn't it have been great to hear her stories about Jesus?

The Bible tells us that Jesus was born of a virgin. That certainly makes Him unique. If that had not actually happened, then Dr. Luke or someone like him could have refuted it with some degree of credibility. He could have at least hedged his bets by simply leaving it out of his book. Instead, Luke placed it right at the beginning where it couldn't be missed.

Taken together, these four accounts provide an indisputably accurate and strikingly complete picture of who Jesus was and what He said about Himself.

The Claims of Christ

So what did Jesus say about Himself? A look at the personal claims of Christ as recorded in the four Gospels will reveal that they really are quite unusual. These four credible accounts record Jesus making statements like: "Believe in God, believe also in me," "I am the way, the truth and the life. No one comes to the Father except through me," "If you knew me, you would know my Father," and "Whoever has seen me has seen the Father."

And after He was arrested, when Jesus was dragged before the high priest, He was asked a point-blank question: "Are You the Christ, the Son of the Blessed One?" ("Christ" is the Greek form of the Hebrew word "Messiah" so what the priest was really asking was: Are you the Jewish Messiah?) How did Jesus answer that direct question? He said: "I am; and you shall see the SON OF MAN SITTING AT THE RIGHT HAND OF POWER, and COMING WITH THE CLOUDS OF HEAVEN" (Mark 14:61-62, the capitalized words are Jesus quoting Messianic prophecy from Psalm 110 and Daniel 7).

Sounds pretty incredible doesn't it? Jesus claimed to be one with God. He claimed to be *the* way to God, not just *a* way to God. He claimed to be *the* truth, not just *a* truth, *the* life, not just *a* life. Then, to top it all off, Jesus told the Jewish High Priest that yes, indeed, He was the long awaited Jewish Messiah.

But that's not all. Throughout the four Gospels we see Jesus doing other things that no normal human being in his or her right mind would ever do. They include:

- Making statements in which He claimed that He was the fulfillment of many other significant Old Testament prophecies. Jesus claimed that the sacred, holy, ancient Jewish Scriptures actually pointed directly to Him.

- Accepting the worship of many who fell down at His feet. He accepted what should only have been given to God.

- Forgiving people of their sins, not just sins committed against Him, but all their sins. That's an authority only God can claim.

- Saying that on judgment day He would be the one to decide the fate of all. That's definitely something only God could do.

At this point, someone may very well ask, "What are you trying to say? What does this mean?"

C.S. Lewis pointed out that anyone who made these kinds of claims would have to be one of three things: a liar, a lunatic, or the Lord Himself. To use another alliteration, the claims of Christ show Him to be either a deceiver, deluded, or the Divine One. There really isn't much else you can say of someone who claims to be God. He would have to be an arrogant, out-and-out con artist, a liar of the worst kind or a certifiable nut-case, a completely deluded megalomaniac with no concept of reality. And if any of these cases are true, then the real Jesus of history should not be taken seriously at all. Both He and His ideas belong locked up and silenced forever.

On the other hand, if none of those explanations fit, then we must conclude that He was who He claimed to be, the Lord Himself. And if that is the case, then Jesus and His message deserve to be taken quite seriously indeed.

In John's Gospel, Jesus is called the "Word" of God, as in the *living* Word or the Word become *flesh*. This past year, my wife and I received a Christmas card from some friends which said it well: "The Word did not become a philosophy, a theory, or a concept to be discussed, debated, or pondered. But the Word became a person to be known, followed, enjoyed, and loved."

Jesus was a real person who did some incredible things that can only be explained if one is willing to accept the claims He made about Himself. When Jesus claimed that He was both God and man to the Jewish religious leaders, they thought this was nothing short of blasphemy. And if Jesus had not been God in the flesh, they would have been right. But the fact remains that everything Jesus did confirmed that He was who He said He was.

Since the days Jesus walked the earth, many people have thought of Him as a great prophet or priest. Even most of the non-Christian religions of the world acknowledge Jesus Christ as a great teacher. But as we have seen, the real Jesus of history did not think of Himself that way. Neither did the writers of the New Testament. And for two centuries, the overwhelming consensus of Christian thought has been that Jesus is much more than a great teacher.

No other major religious leader or philosopher has made the kinds of claims Jesus made. Quoting C.S. Lewis again:

> There is no parallel in other religions. If you had gone to Buddha and asked him, "Are you the son of Bramah?" he would have said, "My son, you are still in the vale of illusion." If you had gone to Socrates and asked, "Are you Zeus?" he would have laughed at you. If you had gone to Mohammed and asked, "Are you Allah?" he would first have rent his clothes and then cut your head off.[6]

Jesus was truly unique. Even His mission bears that out.

The Mission of Christ

The mission of Christ was stated very clearly by the angel who came to explain to Joseph why Mary, his fiancée and still a virgin, had turned up pregnant. The angel said:

> Joseph, son of David, do not be afraid to take Mary as your wife; for that which has been conceived in her is of the Holy Spirit. And she will bear a Son; and you shall call His name Jesus, for it is He who will *save His people from their sins* (Matthew 1:20-21, emphasis added).

Then later on, Jesus Himself stated His mission with great clarity: "For the Son of Man has come *to seek and to save* that which was lost" (Luke 19:10) and "the Son of Man did not come to be served, but *to serve, and to give his life a ransom for many*" (Matthew 20:28, emphasis added). This was reiterated by the apostle Paul who said, "It is a trustworthy statement, deserving full acceptance, that *Christ Jesus came into the world to save sinners*, among whom I am foremost of all" (1 Timothy 1:15, emphasis added).

Without a doubt, the primary mission of Jesus was to come into the world to die for the sins of mankind, to save us from having to face the judgment of God on our own merits. Portrayals of Jesus as just another prophet, priest, or moral teacher simply fall short of recognizing this.

Jesus did not come just to teach us how to love each other more, although He did do that as well. Jesus did not come just to call us to become social activists, to rise up and counter the inequities of this world, although He did teach that we are to be responsible agents of God's resources and that we should share with anyone who is in need. Jesus did not come just to help us get in touch with ourselves or free our inner child, although He did say that we must have the humble faith of a child to enter His kingdom.

Jesus came for the primary and expressed purpose of voluntarily laying down His life as a sacrifice for ours, to pay the price for our sin, to purchase our salvation, and to satisfy the holiness of God. Jesus came so that by His grace, you and I may enter into an eternal relationship with the living God. If you read the New Testament, there is just no mistaking this fact.

Theologians refer to this act—Christ paying for the sins of the world—as the "Atonement." It is an act of God's grace, the giving of a gift which cannot be earned. And it is offered freely to all who believe. This is where we get to the heart of the uniqueness of Jesus Christ.

This teaching is unique among the religions in the world. Christianity promises that forgiveness and mercy are available to all who call upon the name of the Lord. It is not offered on the basis of our merit or obedience, but solely on the merit of Christ's death on the cross.

Not only do the claims of Christ and mission of Christ show Him to be unique in all of history, the message of Christ echoes His uniqueness.

The Message of Christ

What did Jesus teach and preach? Was it only about love? Was it just a feel-good message encouraging us to do random acts of kindness? Can the message of Christ be reduced to a simplistic tolerance? Let's look at what Jesus actually said.

The first passage in which we read of Jesus preaching reveals the essence of His overall message: "Repent, for the kingdom of heaven is at hand" (Matthew 4:17).

That's certainly not the recommended way to start a preaching career. The very first recorded words of Jesus break all accepted public speaking rules. What happened to opening with a "warm the crowd up" humorous anecdote or a feel-good human interest story? But that's not Jesus' style. He begins His ministry by telling everyone they need to repent. He says there is something wrong with us, and we all need to be changed, shaken up, and turned around. Not exactly a page out of *How to Win Friends and Influence People,* is it?

So what does this word *repent* mean that stands in such a central position, right at the beginning of the message of Jesus Christ? The Greek word used in the New Testament is *metanoia,* and it means to have a change of mind that institutes a change in life. Repentance has both a reflective and an active side.

The reflective side means recognizing that we really are sinners and coming to the place in our lives where we feel remorse for our sin. It means understanding that the reason we feel guilty for some of the things we have done is because we really *are* guilty. It's coming to the place where we stop passing the blame, stop offering God our lame excuses, and admit our faults. Each of us has broken God's laws. When we finally stop trying to deny it, we've taken the first step of repentance.

Contrary to what pop-psychology teaches, guilt is not always a bad thing. Guilt is good when it tells you the truth about yourself so that you can begin to face reality and do something about it. You and I cannot find forgiveness if we live in a narcissistic fairyland, denying that we ever do anything wrong.

Repentance also has an active side to it. True repentance is doing something about what you say you believe. We are not predetermined or preprogrammed to do wrong by factors such as genetics, environment, or circumstances, which are out of our control. Jesus' summon to repentance speaks about human dignity, showing us we are not subject to our animalistic tendencies, and calling us to something higher than mere intellectual assent or some kind of emotional experience. It calls us not to be *hearers* of Jesus' message only but to also become *doers* of His message.

According to Jesus, repentance is a prerequisite for entrance into the kingdom of heaven. If a person will not repent, that person cannot enter the kingdom of heaven. That's drawing a line in the sand and asking us on which side of the line we will stand. If you repent, you stand with Christ. If you will not repent, you stand alone. On the reflective side, if a person will not admit his or her need, that person won't recognize his or her need for Christ. On the active side, if a person will not turn away from his or her sin, that person has not truly repented.

To put it another way, if people will not look up to God, they will miss it when God reaches down to them with the free gift of forgiveness. Repentance and forgiveness begin with humility, with bowing before the living God. We must bow intellectually, we must bow morally, and we must bow spiritually. Then by His grace, God takes care of the rest. This is the essence of the unique message of Christ.

In addition to the claims of Christ, the mission of Christ, and the message of Christ, the impact of Christ also speaks of His uniqueness in history.

The Impact of Christ

How can anyone explain the impact of this poor carpenter-turned-rabbi? How is it that the Western calendar came to turn on His life? How is it that 2,000 years later artistic renditions of His face still grace the covers of major news magazines around the world? How do you explain the fact that nearly a third of the world's population identify themselves as His followers by calling themselves Christians?

Nowadays, some people think that faith should be a private affair, something they should keep to themselves. Fortunately that has not always been the case. Since the time of Christ, the contents and ideas found in His teachings have had a profound impact on millions who have come into contact with them. In addition to their personal impact, the fundamental truths of His teachings have provided the motivation behind significant humanitarian and social justice efforts led by such notable personalities as William Wilberforce, Martin Luther King, Jr., and Mother Teresa.

Because of his specifically Christian convictions, Wilberforce led the abolitionist movement in England to rid the world of the scourge of slavery. Because of his specifically Christian convictions, Martin Luther King, Jr., founded the Southern Christian Leadership Conference and became a key figure in the civil rights movement in the United States. Because of her specifically Christian convictions, Mother Teresa of Calcutta worked among the sick and poor of India, which gained her the respect of the Nobel prize committee and even the cynical press corps from around the world.

Wilberforce, King, Mother Teresa, and countless others have all taken their lead from the real Jesus of history. They've followed His example in spite of the costs and inconveniences involved. They've laid down their lives for others, as Jesus taught: "Greater love has no one than this, that one lay down his life for his friends" (John 15:13).

But make no mistake about it, Jesus also had an impact on everyday people like you and me. Many of His best friends were ragtag, uneducated fishermen. But after they met Him, their lives were transformed and they rocked the world with the message of the gospel.

When Jesus walked the earth He healed many who were sick, yet in the lives of the people Jesus healed, He was more than a physical healer. The Gospels tell the story of a man who was hiding behind a tree beside the road one afternoon. He was the picture of death—full of disease, wrapped in scrap cloth and bandages, wheezing, and coughing. When he saw the crowd coming his way, he stumbled out from behind the tree and approached the man in front, the man they called Jesus.

The crowd gasped in horror. Most shrank back to avoid contact. Some turned their heads in revulsion at the hideous man wrapped in bloody rags. Some even picked up rocks, preparing to drive the man away. But before they could, the man fell down in front of Jesus. With a raspy voice he garbled out these words: "Lord, if you are willing, you can make me clean."

At that moment, all eyes shifted to Jesus to see what He would do. And it was then that Jesus did the unthinkable. Matthew, who was there that day, tells us: "Jesus stretched out His hand and touched him" (Matthew 8:3).

The crowd was even more shocked now. Touching a leper was forbidden. Even the disciples must have cringed in horror. Why did Jesus do this? It was against Jewish law. The man was declared unclean. Why did Jesus risk contracting this horrible illness? Didn't He care about His own well-being?

There is no other disease which so isolates a person from the rest of humanity as leprosy. This man had no hope of getting better, he was just waiting for the end. His was a cold and hollow existence void of any human affection. There was no physician on earth who could help him. But Jesus extended His hands and touched this man. One Bible commentator explains that the Greek verb translated here "to touch" was more than just a glancing touch. It is more like "the kind of grip you need when you're pulling someone up from dangling over a cliff."

This touch included something the man had not experienced in years—the full embrace of another human being. Any leper would have been thrilled to have been cleansed with just a word or by washing in some kind of miracle water, but Jesus went beyond all that. He became personally involved.

Jesus didn't see just a leper. Jesus saw a man. Perhaps a husband and father, someone who had not hugged his wife or held his daughter in years. How the man's heart must have ached. The decay in his body must have reflected the horrible decay eating away at his heart.

And then Jesus touched him.

I can't wait until I get home to heaven and I can sit down and talk with that man. I'll bet that day is still as vivid in his memory as if it had happened just yesterday. While it is significant that Jesus healed the man's disease, it is just as significant that He also healed the man's lonely heart. And we never forget experiences like that.

What's So Special About Jesus?

The questions about Jesus must always come down to these: What do you make of Him? Who is Jesus Christ to you? Is your soul in need of His healing touch? Just like the leprous man, all you need do is fall down at Jesus' feet, acknowledge your need, and ask for cleansing.

There has never been anyone like Jesus. Having made the claims He did about Himself, having come to die for our sins, having challenged us to see the honest truth about ourselves, and having inspired and motivated so many people to want to be like Him—only God could have done all of this.

The writer of the New Testament book entitled Hebrews said it this way:

> God, after He spoke long ago to the fathers in the prophets in many portions and in many ways, in these last days has spoken to us in His Son, whom He appointed heir of all things, through whom also He made the world. And He is the radiance of His glory and the exact representation of His nature, and upholds all things by the word of His power (Hebrews 1:1-3).

That's what's so special about Jesus.

- *Is doubt a sin?*

- *Can you be a believer and still have doubts?*

- *What is the best way to go about handling doubt?*

- *Where can we go for answers to our questions and doubts?*

- *How does God feel about our doubts?*

7

How Should We Handle Doubt?

Doubt is not always a sign that a man is wrong; it may be a sign that he is thinking.

—*Oswald Chambers*

What's in a Name?

In case you hadn't noticed, my last name is Thomas. It is the name given me by my immediate ancestors, but it's also long been attached to and joined with the word "doubting" when talking about those who struggle with belief.

It is safe to say that I live up to my name in regard to both of these uses. There are things about me that remind people of the Thomases who've gone before me—my father, grandfather, and other Thomas family members. And there have also been times when my heart and mind were racked by the riddles of life, making it feel as though my faith was choking in a smoke cloud of skepticism.

The moniker "Doubting Thomas" stems from the first century, when a newly resurrected Jesus Christ showed up at a meeting of some of His disciples. Unfortunately, the one named Thomas wasn't there that night. Later, when the disciples told Thomas the good news about having seen Jesus alive again, the incredulous Thomas (who was more of a "seeing is believing" kind of guy) told them, "Unless I shall see in His hands the imprint of the nails, and put my finger into the place of the nails, and put my hand into His side, I will not believe" (John 20:25).

The truth, I've learned, is that even when I'm living up to that side of my Thomas name, I'm not alone. As a matter of fact, according to the Bible, I'm in some pretty good company. Within its pages I've discovered many people of faith who had moments of doubt. It all started in the beginning with Adam and Eve doubting what God had said about the consequences of eating from the Tree of the Knowledge of Good and Evil. They doubted God, picked the fruit, ate it, and the world hasn't been the same since. Doubt is also evident in the lives of people like Abraham, Moses, Gideon, King David, Elijah, and many others, who all went through periods of questioning but nonetheless would all easily qualify for induction into the Hall of Fame for Giants of the Faith.

Most of us have experienced doubts about God. They bring on thoughts such as: If God would just make Himself visible, then all my doubts would disappear. But then it dawns on you that even though God walked the earth in the person of Jesus Christ, living right there in front of humanity, preaching, teaching, and working miracles, there were still those who struggled with doubt.

Thomas was one of them. As one of the original 12 disciples, he had seen Jesus heal people, calm storms, raise the dead, and walk on water right before his very eyes. Yet Thomas still had doubts. It is fair to deduce then, that belief in God and acceptance of the Christian faith is not something that you do once for all and then you are done with it. Christian faith is an everyday affair. It was never meant to be a static, intellectual acquiescence but rather a dynamic belief based on a living relationship.

Maintaining faith is not that much different from having to tune my guitar. Though they tuned it at the factory and the guys at the store where I bought it tuned it again, that wasn't the end of it. I still have to tune the guitar on a regular basis if it is to play correctly. And there is something called "concert pitch," which serves as the standard to which I must tune my guitar if it is to play in *true tune*. So, too, belief must be maintenanced if it is to remain "in tune." And just as I make adjustments on my guitar to get it to concert pitch, there is a living Absolute to whom I must adjust my beliefs if I am to be in tune with *truth*.

How about you? Do you also have times when all this talk about God, Jesus, sin, salvation, and heaven just seems like a bunch of hot air? Do you ever find it just a little too much to believe? If so, I want you to know you're not alone, you're not crazy. If anything, you're at least as normal as I am (that's *supposed* to be a comforting thought).

One significant New Testament personality who learned this was John the Baptist. John, usually considered the last of the Old Testament prophets, was very close to Jesus. They were even relatives and most likely played together as young boys. Yet John the Baptist still struggled with doubts. I think we can learn a lot by looking at his life and his "bout with doubt."

It's important for you to know that John the Baptist probably wouldn't have fit well in an ad for Abercrombie and Fitch, Gap, Eddie Bauer, or Banana Republic. He was a scruffy kind of guy, an outdoorsy type. We're told that he wore camel's hair clothes, lived out in the desert, and ate wild locust and honey. John probably had a matted, sticky beard full of locust shells and grasshopper wings.

Matthew's Gospel tells us that John preached in the wilderness area of Judea; the essence of John's message was the same as that of Jesus: "Repent, for the kingdom of heaven is at hand"(see Matthew 3:1-12).

John's message may have been simple, but it was powerful. We're told that while he was preaching and baptizing, John attracted huge crowds, including some of the religious leaders from Jerusalem—and those guys didn't go out to hear just *anybody*. But John was like a spiritual lightning bolt. He offended almost everyone and spoke the truth like nobody had for quite some time.

John didn't hesitate to "call it like he saw it" when he compared the religious leaders of his time to a bunch of snakes. No one had ever done that. The Pharisees, scribes, and Sadducees were revered as the most holy and religious men around and yet here came this scruffy, uneducated, ragamuffin preacher, John the Baptizer, scolding them like whipped puppies. Then, to add insult to insult, John told the religious leaders that their judgment was right around the corner. He told them that the Messiah would come soon and execute judgment on them, bringing them down because of their fruitless faith and self-righteous hypocrisy.

The highlight of John's ministry was the day he had the privilege of baptizing Jesus (see Matthew 3:13-17). John knew Jesus was the Messiah, the One whose arrival he had been sent to announce. Matthew tells us:

> After being baptized, Jesus went up immediately from the water; and behold, the heavens were opened, and he saw the Spirit of God descending as a dove, and coming upon Him, and behold, a voice out of the heavens, saying, "This is My beloved Son, in whom I am well-pleased" (Matthew 3:16-17).

I don't know about you, but that never happened to me at church camp. We had some great moments singing around the campfire but certainly nothing like that! I'd love to have been there to hear that voice out of heaven. You'd think that anyone who had been there that day would never have had another doubt about God or Jesus. I mean seeing and hearing is believing, right?

Wrong.

When we pick up John's story a few months later, he has been locked up in a dark and damp prison cell.

Why was John in prison? Mark's Gospel tells us that John had openly rebuked King Herod for having an adulterous relationship with his own brother's wife, Herodias. Of course it's never safe to publicly scold an Eastern despot. But John the Baptist was not one to shrink back from the duties of a prophet.

Plus, John probably expected that Jesus hhad come to break him out of prison. After all, the Messiah had come to set up His kingdom, right? Surely freeing John would be high on the Messiah's "Things to Do" list.

But sitting there in that damp and lonely prison for a day, then a week, then a month, and as some have suggested, as much as a year...what do you think was going on in John's mind? Matthew tells us:

> Now when John [the Baptist] in prison heard of the works of Christ, he sent word by his disciples, and said to Him, "Are You the Expected One, or shall we look for someone else?" (Matthew 11:2-3).

Notice Matthew's use of the word "Christ" here. It is most intentional. Matthew wants us to know who it is that John is having doubts about. He's having doubts about Jesus, the same person he had baptized that day with all the fanfare from heaven, the same one he really believed was the Messiah.

Now, if Matthew's Gospel was written to convince us all to believe in Jesus, why in the world would he include an account like this in his book? I mean this is the story of how John, a great man of faith, struggled with doubts about whether Jesus was the Christ.

This is one of the reasons I love the Bible so much. It is honest and realistic. John doubted and Matthew didn't try to spin it, he didn't try to hide it, he was honest about it. God knew that you and I might have questions and doubts, that sometimes our lives feel like we are trapped in some prison, with little to no hope of getting out, feeling as though God was ignoring our circumstances and refusing to come to our rescue. He knew that some of us would have intellectual questions about our faith that would twist our minds into all kinds of contortions, wondering whether God even exists, or if He does, whether He hears our prayers, whether He knows the things we are feeling as we go through those dark nights of the soul.

And so God inspired Matthew to tell the *whole* truth, to include this account, to remind you and I that we aren't that much different from one of the greatest people of faith who ever lived, John the Baptist.

The Doubts of a Prophet

I wonder if there have been times in your life when God didn't perform as you had expected? Times when you thought you'd been completely forgotten by Him? Moments when your faith seemed as thin as a spider's web, so fragile you feared it would not be able to hold the weight of your doubts. Or maybe you made some move in your life thinking you were doing the right thing—just what God wanted you to—and then something went wrong and blew up in your face, causing you to ask: "God, didn't I hear you correctly on this?"

Unfortunately, most of us haven't had the benefit of hearing a voice from heaven like John did. But the point is that even if we did, would we be able to build a lifetime of unwavering faith on a one-time experience? I think it's incredibly important that you and I notice that John the Baptist could not. And if John couldn't, I don't think you and I can either.

As we see from John's life, the strength of our faith is not found in ourselves. It's not about how much faith you have in terms of volume or quantity. It's not about drumming up a level of emotional confidence. It's not about setting your mind on a fixed course and refusing all doubt. It's more often about having a humble and honest heart, one that admits its weakness and looks to God for refreshment and strength. It's about recognizing that the *object* of our faith (Jesus) is also the *source* of our faith (see Hebrews 12:2).

What to Do with Your Doubts

So what did John the Baptist do with his doubts? First, he clarified the core questions. Sometimes when we're going through a period of doubt, it's hard to put a finger on what it is we're questioning. That's why it's good to do what John did. He reduced whatever feelings of doubt he had down to the question about whether or not Jesus was the promised Messiah.

Your questions might be altogether different from John's, but it will still help if you stop, take a few minutes, and figure out exactly what it is you are doubting. Is it the truthfulness of the Bible? Is it whether or not God exists? Is it a question about hypocrisy in the church? Or are you wrestling with whether or not something you are doing is forbidden in Scripture? Identifying your questions is an important first step.

Second, John took his questions straight to Jesus. Although he was in prison and couldn't go himself, he had his disciples take the questions directly to Jesus. He didn't go to the local synagogue officials. He didn't go to the local Self-Help Clinic or call the Jerusalem Psychic Hotline. John went straight to Jesus.

Likewise, it is important to understand that God desires you to come to Him with your honest questions. The Christian faith is not a lifeless religion, it's a relationship with the living God.

The Christian faith does not require you to go to an intermediary—some sort of spiritual guru or mystic philosopher. The Christian faith teaches us that you and I have direct access to the God of the universe, to whom we can both deliver our questions and ask for help.

Now please don't misunderstand me. I'm not trying to say you should never talk with someone else about your doubts. There is much that can be gained from seeking the wise counsel of others. But I *am* saying that biblical Christianity opens the door for you to take your honest questions right into the throne room of the Almighty God. King David knew this well when in a moment of doubt and honest desperation he prayed "How long, O LORD? Wilt thou forget me for ever? How long wilt thou hide thy face from me?" (Psalm 13:1 RSV).

Whenever you have doubts, no matter how intense they might seem, your best course of action is to clarify your core questions and then go straight to God with them.

Don't worry too much about how you word your questions. David never did. He shook his fist at heaven all the time. He expressed deep doubts about God's love for him and about God's timing in bringing about the help he needed. And in this humble honesty before God, David was called a "man after God's own heart." What an honor to be remembered that way.

Finally, we should see our lives in the context of God's plans for us. This is what John the Baptist did. He knew that God had plans for his life that went way beyond his own imagination. He knew that the very God who was in charge of all of human history had a hand on his life.

We can trust the sovereign Lord of all with our doubts. He is not afraid of our questions; He is not insulted by our fears. God in His infinitude has numbered the very hairs of your head, and He knows what you are going through. The reason you are safe is because, in the end, you are in His hands.

How God Responds to Our Doubts

Matthew continues to describe what happened that day:

> Jesus answered and said to them, "Go and report to John what you hear and see: the BLIND RECEIVE SIGHT and the lame walk, the lepers are cleansed and the deaf hear, the dead are raised up, and the POOR HAVE THE GOSPEL PREACHED TO THEM" (Matthew 11:4-5; the words in capitals are excerpted paraphrases from Isaiah 35 and 61).

How did Jesus answer John's questions? By pointing to the miracles He was performing and the message He was preaching. Both of these tied Jesus to Old Testament messianic prophecy. Jesus reminded John that the truth he was seeking had been revealed in Scripture and in the midst of John's doubts and troubles, it was the Word of the Lord that would sustain him.

King David also knew about the power of God's Word to sustain us during tough times; listen to how he put it:

> Deal bountifully with Thy servant, that I may live and keep Thy word. Open my eyes, that I may behold wonderful things from Thy law. I am a stranger in the earth; do not hide Thy commandments from me. My soul is crushed with longing after Thine ordinances at all times. Thou dost rebuke the arrogant, the cursed, who wander from Thy commandments. Take away reproach and contempt from me, for I observe Thy testimonies. Even though princes sit and talk against me, Thy servant meditates on Thy statutes. Thy testimonies also are my delight; they are my counselors (Psalm 119:17-24).

How much more is this true for us? We have the benefit of looking back through Scripture, both the Old Testament and the New Testament, and learning how these great people of faith struggled with doubt. In the midst of much worse life conditions than any of us will probably ever face, they came face to face with the giant of doubt. And what was it that sustained them? What was it that gave them comfort? The statutes of God and the testimonies of God's faithfulness. These became their counselors, their words of comfort and peace that restored their confidence in God's love for them.

When we have periods of doubt, one of the best things we should do is one of the simplest things we can do. Read God's Word. Find a passage that speaks to the circumstances you are wrestling with. Find a narrative passage that describes how someone else dealt with a similar situation.

Read it once, and then read it again. Meditate on it. Pray and ask the Holy Spirit to reveal its words of hope to you. In humility, invite the Lord to open the eyes of your heart and show you how his Word can be a lamp unto *your* feet and a light unto *your* path right here, right now.

Finishing the Race

John had an incredible start in faith and Jesus counseled him by saying, "Don't give up now, don't stumble by misunderstanding Me or My timing in bringing about My will for your life." I think that God has said the same thing to me, and perhaps He is saying that to you right now for whatever doubts might be unsettling your mind and heart. Don't give up. Don't doubt in the dark what you knew to be true in the light. God will prove Himself to be faithful. The only question is: Will you trust Him?

Adam, Eve, Abraham, Moses, Gideon, King David, Elijah, John the Baptist, you, and me. All of us are believers and sometimes doubters. Our walk of faith reminds me of Derek Redmond. In the official record books of the 1992 Olympics, Derek Redmond's attempt in the semifinals of the men's 400 meter race is listed as "race abandoned." But as *USA Today's* Mike Dodd has said: "To 65,000 fans in Montjuic Olympic Stadium in Barcelona, Spain, and millions of television viewers, that's the most ironic misnomer in the history of the Games."

I remember watching that race on television. It's one of those moments you just never forget. Redmond was 250 meters away from the finish line when he pulled a hamstring and fell down hard.

He knew he wasn't just another runner, he really had a chance at the medal. But then he fell down.

As the other runners blew past him, Redmond said that he thought to himself, "If I get up now and run, I can still qualify." He struggled to his feet, grimaced in pain, and stumbled forward several more feet. But then he fell down again.

By now, the other runners had all crossed the finish line. But as the cameras retrained their focus from the finish line to the runner who was once again rising to his feet, it became apparent that the race was far from over.

Seconds turned into minutes, almost in slow motion as Redmond took one step and then another. But to the horror of the watching world, it quickly became evident that he would never make it on his own.

Then all of a sudden, there was a stirring in the crowd. From somewhere near the top of the stands, another man came running down. He jumped over the concrete divider and headed toward the fallen Olympian. Arriving at the runner's side, he threw his arm around the young man's shoulder to support him. The young runner seemed dazed at first and tried to pull away but the man wouldn't let go. Then the man said to him "Son, you don't have to do this. You've got nothing to prove." And Derek Redmond knew who it was that had come to his aid.

As Dodd reported their conversation, it went something like this.

Derek recalled, "I told him I had to finish; I was going to finish the race."

Then Jim Redmond, Derek's father said, "Well, we've started everything together. We'll finish this together."

The two walked slowly all the way to the finish line together; all over the world, people did exactly what the 65,000 people in that stadium did that day…we stood with cheerful applause at the courage and perseverance of Derek Redmond who finished his race.

Doubt is a little like pulling a muscle in the middle of your race. Sometimes it hits you from out of nowhere, like being blindsided by a personal tragedy or finding out that one of the people you look up to is not all he or she appeared to be.

At other times, doubt can be the result of the slow atrophy of your faith, like when a muscle hasn't been used in a while. Spiritual atrophy happens when we don't spend time with the Father, meditate on God's Word, pray more than just crisis prayers, give ourselves away in service, or focus our hearts in true and spiritual worship of God.

John the Baptist had fallen into doubt when he wasn't very far from the finish line. And the Father, looking down from heaven, made sure that he got the encouraging news he needed. Jesus was indeed the Coming One.

Frederick Buechner has said, "Whether your faith is that there is a God or that there is not a God, if you don't have any doubts you are either kidding yourself or asleep."[7] Let's not try to fool ourselves, God, or each other. Let's be honest about doubt. And above all, let's not be guilty of falling down and then just falling asleep where we fell. Let's keep our faith moving.

If you are going through a period of doubt, consider yourself among those of us who fall down once in awhile. To doubt is not to sin. Honest doubt is one thing, willful disbelief is quite another. One is sincerity; the other is obstinacy. One hungers for light; the other falls asleep in the dark.

Take courage. Your doubts could just be a sign that you are thinking, and your faith is getting ready to start moving again. And remember to do what John the Baptist did: clarify your core questions, take them straight to God, then begin to see your life as a part of God's overall plan. Finally, go to God's Word for light and guidance.

Then you can say with David:

> I have chosen the faithful way; I have placed Thine ordinances before me. I cleave to Thy testimonies; O LORD, do not put me to shame! I shall run the way of Thy commandments, for Thou wilt enlarge my heart (Psalm 119: 30-32).

- If God is both good and all powerful, then why does He allow all of the evil, pain, suffering, and death in the world?

- Why do bad things happen to good people and good things happen to bad people?

- Where is God when life hurts?

- Can we find meaning or purpose in our pain or make any sense out of all the tragedy in this life?

8

Why Does God Allow So Much Pain and Suffering?

When pain is to be borne, a little courage helps more than much knowledge, a little human sympathy more than much courage, and the least tincture of the love of God more than all.

—*C.S. Lewis*

HORATIO G. SPAFFORD WAS A SUCCESSFUL Chicago businessman who, at the age of 43, suffered a major financial setback due to the Great Chicago Fire of 1871. He and his wife were still reeling from the recent death of their son and so, after the fire, Spafford decided the family needed to get away for awhile. His good friend D.L. Moody was about to hold a series of evangelistic crusades in England, so Spafford and his wife decided to book passage on a ship to take the family over and join Moody.

At the very last minute, Spafford had to stay behind to attend to some unexpected business developments but he sent his wife and four daughters on ahead, planning to follow as soon as he could.

On November 22, as their ship, the *S.S. Ville du Havre,* was crossing the Atlantic, it was struck by an English vessel called the *Lochearn.* The *Ville du Havre* sank in just 12 minutes and 226 lives were lost. When the survivors landed at Cardiff, Wales, Mrs. Spafford sent this cable message to her husband: "Saved alone."

Spafford booked passage on the very next ship to go and join his grieving wife. As he crossed the Atlantic, the captain pointed out the place where the *Ville du Havre* had gone down. That night, Spafford penned these words to a now famous hymn of the faith:

> When peace like a river attendeth my way,
> When sorrows like sea-billows roll;
> Whatever my lot, Thou hast taught me to say,
> "It is well, it is well, with my soul."

In short duration, Spafford suffered the loss of his son, financial ruin in the great fire, and then the loss of his four daughters. Humanly speaking, it is almost impossible to imagine how anyone could find peace in the midst of such a relentless string of tragedies. What was it that Horatio Spafford held onto during those times of such great personal pain and loss? What was it he believed in so strongly that gave him such invincible hope?

The subject of pain, evil, and suffering has been the study of philosophers and theologians for centuries. The question of why God allows pain and suffering has probably crossed your mind as well. Most likely it arose when you or someone you know was going through some kind of tragedy or painful experience. That's when we are most likely to ask the big "why" questions. *Why* did this happen? Why did this happen to *me?* Why did this happen *now?* And that's when we are most desperate to find some meaning behind our suffering.

It may not lessen anyone's pain to point out that the problem of pain is not a new issue. Even when we look to the Bible we read that Jesus said to His followers: "In the world you have tribulation, but take courage; I have overcome the world" (John 16:33). You'll notice that Jesus did not say *if* you have tribulation. He said you *will* have tribulation. However, according to Jesus, while pain is a given, misery is optional. When tribulation comes in this world, Jesus said we could take courage because He has overcome the world.

At this point, someone may say, "That's nice, but could you help me see precisely *how* Jesus' overcoming the world will help me? Why doesn't God just wave His magic wand over the world and end all the evil, pain, and suffering? How are we supposed to find the silver lining behind some of these massive thunderclouds?"

To be sure, pain is everywhere, and it comes in all shapes and sizes. Pain comes wrapped in earthquakes, tornadoes, flooding, disease, drunk-driving accidents, high school gunfire, church burnings, divorce, political corruption, and so on. It seems indiscriminate about who its victims are. Babies and children aren't innocent or cute enough to escape its reach, marriages aren't sacred enough, churches and synagogues aren't holy enough, post offices and other government buildings aren't protected enough. Pain can walk through any door, anywhere, at anytime, and pull the rug out from under even the safest of the safe.

Two Kinds of Pain

The first thing we should realize is that there are at least two general categories of pain: physiological and psychological. The first manifests itself in physical pain, as when you smash your finger with a hammer or break your leg. The second category of pain is experienced in the mental and emotional realm, when, for example, you are afraid of something or your heart is broken by some kind of loss or missed opportunity. Both kinds of pain come in a variety of intensities. It's one thing to burn your finger and quite another to lose a limb. It's one thing to flunk a math test and quite another to lose a job. Sometimes people experience both kinds of pain at the same time, such as when they make a trip to the dentist or have to go to war to defend their country.

Eventually, everyone experiences both kinds of pain. You've probably had one of those days—you know, where everything that *can* go wrong, *does* go wrong. Did one of those days ever turn into one of those weeks? Did that week ever turn into one of those months or years? And did it ever begin to look like it was on its way to becoming one of those lives? If so, then you know what I mean about the universality of pain.

My wife claims to be a natural klutz; she says she can't walk through a store without bumping into something and knocking several items off the shelves. She experiences pain almost daily and bears the proof in the scars on her hand from cutting the pumpkin, scars on her knees from banging into table legs at restaurants, and a scar on her lip from knocking over a microphone stand, stepping on the base of the stand, and then watching in horror as the microphone came back at her like the proverbial "stepped on" grass rake.

Of course these kinds of physical pain are minor compared to what some people have to deal with. There are those who have to cope with debilitating amounts of physical pain every minute of their lives.

Psychological pain is no stranger to most of us either. We've experienced this kind of pain when we take a trip to the doctor, are unsettled by a series of midterm exams, or become tied up in knots at employee review time. The scars of psychological pain include the relational dysfunctions of adult children of alcoholics, the increasing divorce rate, and the exponential growth in the sale of mood-altering drugs.

Emotional pain can be quite traumatic for those who live under the tyranny of a verbally abusive spouse, sibling, or parent. Being told you are a "dummy" and that you "never do anything right" can inflict a devastating amount of pain on the human spirit. Scars of the soul run deep, and the light of life can fade from the eyes of anyone who has received the brunt of life-long psychological pain.

Looking for Hope

There are really two approaches to the discussion of pain. One is intellectual and the other existential. One deals with theories and the other with experiences. A meaningful treatment of the subject must include both aspects. To talk about pain, suffering, and evil on a purely philosophical level would be fine for those who like to chase such things around, but it would leave out some of the richest thoughts ever heard on the subject. And yet, to focus only on personal experiences might make us feel better for a moment or two but then would leave us with nothing to anchor our minds and hearts to when the pain or the memory of it returns.

Besides, the very reasons people are interested in the subject of pain are also both intellectual and existential. They either have experienced some great amount of pain and are trying to make sense out of it, or they are afraid they will soon experience pain and are preparing in advance to take the hit. So, if we are to understand pain at all, we must grapple with it intellectually and then take a look at the role pain plays in the real world of our lives.

The Intellectual Problem of Pain

You might be among those who have taken a philosophy course somewhere along the way which taught that if God exists, He is either unwilling or unable to do something about the evil and suffering in this world. Otherwise, He would surely have done away with all that by now. You might have had discussions centering on a question like: Why would a good God allow the horrors of the Holocaust, the scourges of disease, the death and destruction of war? If He has the power, then why didn't He prevent them from happening in the first place? I believe these are honest questions which deserve honest answers.

We can learn something from the very fact that pain exists. You see, pain can only have meaning if there is something more to this world than just chemicals and atoms. That is, if you are an atheist and you believe that the physical universe is all there is, then you really have no right to complain about the existence or injustice of pain. For the consistent atheist, painful experiences are just the result of time plus chance, accidental collocations of elements of the physical universe. For the true atheist, there is no such thing as finding meaning in what amounts to the natural movements of an impersonal world.

The atheist has both a harder and an easier time explaining the existence of pain than the Christian. If the atheist is talking about the *cause* of pain, the explanation can be that when pain is experienced, it is a result of the movements of various elements of the physical universe. No real intellectual problem exists from this vantage point; everything is mechanistic because everything is meaningless.

But the moment an atheist begins talking about the outrage or injustice of pain or the significance and meaning a person might find in painful experiences, the atheist has begun to cheat on atheism. For the atheist to remain consistent, he or she is forced to admit that the death of a child is as ultimately meaningless as the falling of a rock into the ocean.

The Christian has a much more difficult job in talking about the cause of pain, especially as it relates to the existence of a good and all-powerful God. But Christians do have the upper hand in that they can talk about the injustice of pain and about how to find meaning in pain which the atheist cannot.

The existence of pain is one of the favorite intellectual arguments of the atheist and perhaps the most formidable. The issue is a difficult one to deal with no matter how you approach it. A case can be made that the existence of pain suggests the universe is a dangerous and evil place in which to live. From the very day you were born, you began to die, as though life itself were just a cruel joke—a joke set in play either by "chance" or some kind of sadomasochistic deity who enjoys watching us writhe and squirm our way from birth all the way to the grave.

While this hopeless response is often presented as though it were the *only* solution to the philosophical problem of pain, the issue is not so simply dealt with. The existence of one thing does not disprove the existence of another, nor does it necessarily determine the characteristics of another thing. The existence of pain really says nothing about the existence or character of God. It is not any sort of explicit contradiction to say "God exists" and also to say "pain exists." A contradiction would be if I were to say "God exists" and "God does not exist" or "pain exists" and "pain does not exist." The real question is: How do we make sense out of the coexistence of the two?

Is there a good answer? How can we reconcile the existence of a good and all-powerful God with a meaningful answer to the problem of pain? Part of the answer may be found in uncovering a distorted view of what is meant by the terms "all-powerful" and "good" when we talk about God.

The All-Powerful God

If by "all-powerful" we mean that God can do anything at all, then we are not talking about the Christian idea of God. Anything at all would have to include the ability to create a square circle, a round triangle, a married bachelor, a male daughter, or any number of other absolute impossibilities. But if the words "square" and "circle" have any meaning at all, then God cannot create a square circle.

A common question that is asked is: "If God can do *anything*, can God make a rock so big that He couldn't pick it up?" A similar logical conundrum is: "What happens when an unstoppable force meets an immovable object?" In both cases we are dealing with mutually exclusive alternatives which lead to absolute impossibilities. God is the name of the being who is truly supreme and nothing can be greater than God. God cannot create a rock or anything else that would then be greater than Himself and which would thereby stop Him from being who He is. As for the second question, if there were such a thing as an unstoppable force, there could be no such thing as an immovable object and vice versa. The existence of one negates the existence of the other. Both of these questions are nonsensical because they are dealing with absolute impossibilities.

God is all-powerful, and this means that anything that can be done can be done by God. God can create from out of nothing, manage the universe, divide the heavens from the earth, and raise the dead. There is nothing God cannot do except stop being God.

The Goodness of God

The second thing we need to clarify is what we mean when we say that God is good. If "good" means that God exists to meet our every whim, like a spiritual Santa Claus, then we are not talking about the Christian idea of God at all. When Christians say that God is good, we mean that God has our highest good in mind, that He is benevolent, and that He intends for us to live life to its fullest, experiencing the kind of spiritual growth that will enable us to reflect His image into a world which is full of darkness.

Those who think of God as a magic genie whose only mission is to secure our amusement and happiness have missed the point altogether. God will not sacrifice our holiness for our happiness. Our greatest good, as defined by God, is not about job opportunities, romantic encounters, or a bulging savings account. In and of themselves, these things are not bad. But sometimes we make the mistake of thinking our greatest good is tied directly to these kinds of things. In God's economy, however, our greatest good has more to do with personal holiness and opportunities to accurately reflect God's glory in our world.

One element of God's plan for our greatest good is that we should have free will. With that free will, God has set it up that we can choose to do right or wrong and that there will be consequences that attend our choices. God did not desire to make a world filled with automatons and robots who have no free will. He took the great risk of love and gave us the opportunity to choose or refuse His Lordship in our lives. That necessarily leaves open the possibility that we will separate ourselves from God and from each other by the choices we make. When we do this, we leave ourselves open to the natural consequences which follow our selfishness.

Some have suggested that it would have been better for God not to have given us free will. But as Augustine, one of the greatest philosopher-theologians of the Christian faith, put it, "As a runaway horse is better than a stone which does not run away because it lacks self-movement and sense perception, so the creature is more excellent which sins by free will than that which does not sin only because it has no free will."[8] And even more excellent is the creature who chooses not to sin in a response of love and gratitude to the Almighty and good God.

That God is good does not always mean we will fully understand what God, in His goodness, intends for us. We are finite and affected by the Fall. Our concept of what is good for us is sure to be at times quite different from God's. But not so different as to render the word "good" meaningless, as if God's goodness were a complete opposite to our conception of goodness. As C.S. Lewis has put it:

> The Divine "goodness" differs from ours, but it is not
> sheerly different: it differs from ours not as white from

black but as a perfect circle from a child's first attempt to draw a wheel. But when the child has learned to draw, it will know that the circle it then makes is what it was trying to make from the very beginning.[9]

This means we will not always understand how a good God would allow some of the struggles that we must face. But the further we go along in spiritual growth, the more clearly we see and understand God's dealings with us. He is about the business of improving us, never having been one to settle for the status quo. Like a master painter working on his or her paintings, God dabs, rubs, strokes, and brings into our lives those things which He deems are for our greater good.

The Cause of Pain

From the Christian perspective there is a single primary cause of pain in the world. Pain is a result of what theologians call the Fall of mankind. The Fall refers to the entrance of sin into the physical world, the intentional disregard for God's will which began with our first parents, Adam and Eve. This does not mean that Christians believe each and every specific incident of pain is a direct result of a specific sin, but that the reality of sin is the general cause behind all pain.

Through the Fall, humankind and all of creation have been polluted from the original state in which they were created. Because of Adam and Eve's disobedience, God pronounced a judgment on mankind which theologian Anthony Hoekema[10] has pointed out was threefold. This judgement is described in the third chapter of Genesis.

1) "Cursed is the ground because of you; in toil you shall eat of it all the days of your life" (Genesis 3:17). Hoekema tells us that the word translated "toil" here is the same word as "pains" used to describe the pains of childbirth. Before the Fall, Adam

and Eve had enjoyed their work in the garden but because of the Fall, physical work was now accompanied by pain and difficulty.

2) "Both thorns and thistles it shall grow for you" (Genesis 3:18). Because of the Fall, their labor to grow food to survive became inconvenienced by interruptions and setbacks. Many Bible scholars believe this part of the curse of the Fall extends beyond thorns and thistles, showing up in other aspects of nature such as floods, earthquakes, hurricanes, and diseases. This appears to be confirmed by Romans 8 when the apostle Paul tells us that the whole of creation groans to be "set free from its slavery to corruption." And so we have at least the suggestion that our struggle with nature and natural disasters has come as part of the consequences of the Fall.

3) "For you are dust, and to dust you shall return" (Genesis 3:19). Physical death is also a direct consequence of the Fall. Prior to the Fall, physical death did not exist. According to Genesis 5:5, Adam lived to the ripe old age of 930 and many others back then lived multiple hundreds of years as well. Current life spans are much shorter than they were around the origin of mankind. This is likely a result of the compounding pollution of sinful deeds.

So for the Christian, the general cause of all pain stems directly or indirectly back to the Fall of mankind and the entrance of sin into the world. Before the Fall, things were as God had originally intended. Pain, struggling, and death were clearly not a part of human experience. After the Fall, pain, struggling, and death became a shocking reality for our ancestors and an inherited reality for us.

A World Without Pain?

Some have asked the question: "Why couldn't God come up with another plan, a world where there didn't have to be any pain?"

From the Bible we know that God desired to make mankind with a moral free will. This means God decided to create us with the real opportunity to choose between right and wrong. He placed us in an environment that allowed for these choices to be exercised, accompanied by real consequences. These consequences, whether good or bad, whether pleasurable or painful, are the direct or indirect result of the right and wrong choices we make of our own free will. It would be self-contradictory for God to have created us with free will and then to coerce us into always making right choices in order that we'd only experience good consequences. Therefore, it is reasonable for God to have made our world a place where pain exists and can actually occur.

In the world in which we live, we encounter both *natural laws* and *moral laws* which have been set up by God. Because this is so, our free moral choices now have real weight; they impact the amount of pain we experience and the amount of pain we might cause for others around us.

For instance, in the physical world God made mankind as air-breathing mammals. But if we were to try living underwater without the aid of breathing machinery, it would be logical to expect that we would come to some harm and possibly die. This is part of the *natural law* and covers the natural order of the physical world in which we live. When we go against natural law, we don't just break the natural law, we break ourselves against it.

The same thing is true with moral law. Since God has told us it is wrong for us to murder each other, lie to each other, commit adultery, and so on, our God-given moral significance necessarily includes the real option to choose wrong. So, if we were to choose to disobey God's moral law by committing adultery, we might very well ruin our marriages, causing pain to both ourselves and our spouses. Or if we were to hold another human being under water for an extended period of time, we could, of our own free will, employ the natural law, which God set up, to break a moral law (which God also set up) and inflict real and fatal pain on another human being.

The freedom that comes with moral significance is a freedom that when respected can keep us relatively safe or, when disregarded, can cause us great harm. It would be an absolute impossibility to create a world in which creatures are given true free will and then only permit them to do that which is good so that their lives are completely pleasant.

The Existential Problem of Pain

Now, let's move out of the realm of philosophy and ask some very hard—and very real—questions. Why do babies die? Why are there plane crashes? Why do families break up? Why do there have to be such horrible things as heart attacks, cancer, and AIDS? And why are people so violent and evil toward each other?

At 9:02 A.M. on April 19, 1995, a 4,800-pound truck bomb exploded in front of the Alfred P. Murrah Federal Building in Oklahoma City, killing 168 innocent people and shocking the entire nation. The evil of terrorism had raised its ugly head in America. Just four days later, one of the greatest advocates for faith in God, Reverend Billy Graham, came to stand up at the memorial service for the Oklahoma City bombing victims and try to make sense out of that horrible tragedy. I watched it on television that day and thought: What would he say? What could he say? Shock and disbelief filled the air. Children had died needlessly. Grandmothers and grandfathers were taken away. Many bodies, hearts, and minds would be bruised for the rest of their lives. The hollow emptiness and loneliness which accompanies the loss of loved ones permeated the entire scene. The shock of such an evil act had left our nation stunned.

But as Dr. Graham got up to speak, the mixed tears of grief and hope began to flow. Here, the one person of whom it might rightly be said "he speaks for God," rose to do his duty. My wife and I wept too as we strained to hear every word Dr. Graham would say. When he reached the podium, he told about the questions everyone had asked him: "Why did this happen?" "Why would God have allowed it to happen?"

There was a pause which lasted for what seemed like forever. He then said the three words which disarmed all the critics of the gospel. With a deep and honest sadness in his eyes Graham said, "I don't know."

Like Dr. Graham, we Christians can't always explain why bad things happen. We simply must accept that for some reason, at certain times, God allows us to walk through a dark valley.

But Dr. Graham did not stop there. We don't have to, either. As believers in God, while forced to say, "I don't know to the 'why' of pain," we also have the hopeful joy of being able to say, "But I do know this: When pain comes, because there is a God in heaven who loves us, we do not have to walk through any dark valley alone."

The Suffering God

During World War II the theologian Deitrich Bonhoeffer was jailed by the Nazis because of his faith. From his prison cell he wrote a note describing where he looked for help. It stated, "Only a suffering God can help." What's that he said? A *suffering* God? How could God suffer? *Why* would God ever have to suffer?

Just a casual look at the life of Jesus will show that He suffered through many of the same painful experiences we suffer in this world. Jesus endured both physical pain and emotional pain. His body was broken for us, and He knew what it was like to be ridiculed by cruel people. He knew what it was like to feel betrayed by a close friend and to lose a loved one to physical death. By entering humanity, Christ personally suffered the same kinds of pain that you and I must endure because of the effects of the Fall.

The Christian answer to suffering and pain is that we serve a Suffering God, one who knows what we experience and who has willingly taken upon Himself pain and suffering which were not due to Him. The God of the Bible understands and is able to comfort us because He knows the injustice of pain even better than we do. The pain Jesus experienced was not because of anything He had done but because of what we had done. He died for *our* sin.

God does not ask us to weather a storm that He has not weathered Himself. Dorothy Sayers once said:

> For whatever reason God chose to make man as he is— limited and suffering and subject to sorrows and death—He had the honesty and the courage to take His own medicine. Whatever game He is playing with His creation, He has kept His own rules and played fair. He can exact nothing from man that He has not exacted from Himself. He has Himself gone through the whole of human experience, from the trivial irritations of family life and the cramping restrictions of hard work and lack of money to the worst horrors of pain and humiliation, defeat, despair, and death. When He was a man, He played the man. He was born in poverty and died in disgrace and thought it well worthwhile.[11]

It is in God's plan that one day He will bring suffering to an end. Because Christ was victorious over death, He has dismantled the permanence of death and evil. During our times of pain and suffering He comforts those who know Him and is calling out to those who don't to come to Him for peace and comfort.

We don't know why we have to endure pain and suffering, but we know we don't have to endure it alone. We don't know exactly what God's purposes are in each case, but we can trust that He knows what we are going through and will turn it into something that works for our ultimate good. William Cowper wrote this poem entitled *God Moves in a Mysterious Way.*

God moves in mysterious ways
His wonders to perform;
He plants His footsteps in the sea,
And rides upon the storm.

His purposes will ripen fast,
Unfolding every hour;
The bud may have a bitter taste,
But sweet will be the flower.

Blind unbelief is sure to err,
And scan His works in vain:
God is His own interpreter,
And He will make it plain.

Possible Reasons Behind Specific Instances of Pain and Suffering

I feel a bit hesitant as I write the next few pages because I don't want anyone reading this to think that I am trivializing their pain and suffering by running through a list of possible reasons for why they might be going through what they are going through. But for the sake of helping make some sense of it, I'd like to suggest several possible reasons why God allows specific instances of pain and suffering. Perhaps you will see one that applies to your own life.

Pain Can Be a Step Toward a Greater Good

God's primary goal in our lives is to change us. He is intent on developing the character of Christ in all believers. I often cling to the things of this world so tightly that He has to pry my fingers off them so I will more fully place my trust in Him. There can be pain as I resist. There can be fear because I don't always trust that God knows what He is doing. But in the end, all that happens to me is for the greater good of my becoming more like

Christ. We must remember that just as in dentistry and surgery, sometimes a little pain can lead to a much greater good.

Pain Can Serve as a Warning Device

Pain can sometimes be an effective warning device. It helps protect us by influencing us to withdraw from harmful activity. Physical pain is primarily associated with injury or the threat of injury to our body. We need pain for our own good. Leprosy is a disease in which the human body loses its ability to feel pain. One might think that sounds like a good idea. But if you can't feel pain, your body becomes its own worst enemy. If you can't feel pain, you won't know when you are touching something that will burn your skin or when you have stepped on something that will cut your foot.

Psychological pain, on the other hand, may be a warning to discontinue some activity or attitude in your life. It may be that we are consumed with materialism or popularity, and in the struggle to advance we experience emotional pain. Sometimes God uses this kind of pain to get our attention and warn us that we have set our affections on the wrong things. As C.S. Lewis has said: "God whispers to us in our pleasures, speaks in our conscience, but shouts in our pains: it is His megaphone to rouse a deaf world." And so pain can be a useful tool God uses to warn us of spiritual danger.

Pain Can Help in Soul-Making

The apostle Paul wrote: "We also exult in our tribulations, knowing that tribulation brings about perseverance; and perseverance, proven character; and proven character, hope; and hope does not disappoint" (Romans 5:3-5). And the apostle James wrote: "Consider it all joy, my brethren, when you encounter various trials, knowing that the testing of your faith produces endurance. And let endurance have its perfect result, that you may be perfect and complete, lacking in nothing"

(James 1:2-4). So we see there is a direct correlation between the tribulations we endure in this life and the work of God in perfecting us and developing mature character in us.

This world is a place where outstanding achievement and terrible disaster can both happen. Only in such a world can real soul-making and character development take place.

Pain Helps Increase Our Sense of Purpose and Mission

There is a sense in which we are the hands, feet, and voice of God. For some reason God has chosen to use believers as His agents and the ambassadors of His kingdom as one of the means to accomplish His purposes in this world. Because some people experience pain, others then have real opportunities for heroism. When we help others in need our hearts are enlarged, our lives are enriched, and we begin fulfilling the law of Christ, which is that we should "bear one another's burdens." This in turn inspires others to do the same, and together we reflect the love and mercy of God by being generous through our giving and other philanthropic endeavors.

If you are in a place of being able to give, become heroic in your giving. If you are in need, be humble enough to let people help, and you will enable them to become more like God.

Storms of Correction and Storms of Perfection

The story of Jonah in the Old Testament[12] is an illustration of how God used pain to correct and discipline someone. God told Jonah to go to Nineveh and preach, but Jonah disobeyed and jumped on a boat headed in the other direction. God sent a storm, and Jonah got thrown overboard; he was swallowed by a great fish and remained alive in its belly for three days. While inside the fish, Jonah repented and prayed for God's deliverance and God responded. The fish coughed up Jonah, and then Jonah went to Nineveh and preached, and the people repented.

The intense fear, pain, and suffering that Jonah went through was what you might call a Storm of Correction. God was using pain to correct and discipline his wayward servant.

The story of Jesus' disciples in their boat out on the stormy Sea of Galilee, is what might be called a Storm of Perfection.[13] Jesus was with them in the boat but was asleep. Even though they were professional fishermen, they were frightened by this sudden and violent storm. They cried out to Jesus for help, and He awoke and rebuked the winds and the sea. Immediately it became perfectly calm. Here is an instance of Christ allowing His disciples to go through a time of great fear and anxiety in order to mature their faith and develop their trust in Him as they saw His ability and willingness to respond to their needs.

Pain as Judgment for Specific Sin

There are times when God allows pain as a judgment or punishment for specific sin and rebellion. We saw this with Adam and Eve as they tasted pain, struggle, and death. The story of Jonah is also an example of judgment for his rebellion. In the world, fines and jail sentences act as a deterrent for those who are considering committing crimes. It should be no surprise that God would at times exact punishment from us when we disregard His will in our lives.

But in talking about this, we should take great care, especially when it comes to a discussion of how God may be dealing with any specific case. It is not for any of us to determine when God is or is not meting out punishment for someone else's specific sin. The religious leaders of Jesus' time made the mistake of doing this, and we must learn from their mistake. The only one who has the right to execute judgment and punishment is God Himself. But we should be aware that there are times when God may deal with all of us in this way.

Laws of Nature

Some of the pain that is produced in this world is simply a matter of the normal functioning of the laws of nature. These instances appear gratuitous. When a hurricane rips across Alabama on a Sunday morning and flattens a church where people are worshiping and praying to God, it is very hard to come to terms with what possible good God might have in mind. When earthquakes cause so much death and destruction, it is mind boggling to even try to figure out why God allows them.

For those of us who have never been victims of these kinds of tragic events, the only meaningful way to view them is to find some way that God wants us to respond to the needs of their victims. This is an opportunity for us to exercise heroism, generosity, self-sacrifice, and compassion.

Special Display of God's Glory

On certain occasions in the Scripture, pain and suffering have been allowed by God for no other reason than to permit a special opportunity for God to receive glory. One such instance is found in John chapter 9, where Jesus and His disciples come upon a man who has been blind since birth. The disciples asked Jesus: "Rabbi, who sinned, this man or his parents, that he should be born blind?" Jesus answered by telling the disciples it was neither this man's sin nor his parents' sin, but so that the works of God might be displayed in his life.

Jesus said the same thing on the occasion of His friend Lazarus' death. When the messengers came with the news of Lazarus' being deathly ill, Jesus said: "This sickness is not unto death, but for the glory of God, that the Son of God may be glorified by it" (John 11:4).

The miracles of Jesus both confirmed who He was—the promised Christ—and they showed forth His compassion.

These are instances when God's glory could be visibly displayed in and through tragic circumstances.

How many times have we heard of situations where people have gone through inconceivable pain or suffering but still showed incredible faith and courage in God and His purposes? Sometimes there is healing and sometimes not, but in the end, their unshakable faith in God is a magnificent testimony that brings glory to God.

As Dorothy Sayers has pointed out, God does not always prevent the expression of evil. Sometimes He transforms it. God did not prevent Judas from betraying Christ, but He turned it into an offer of salvation to the world. God did not stop the crown of thorns from being jammed on the head of Jesus, He turned it into a crown of glory. God did not stop Christ's death on the cross, He turned it into a resurrection day.

Direct Effort of Satan to Defeat or Distract Us

In the heavenly realm, we have an enemy. He is the enemy of our spiritual life in God, the enemy of our marriages, and the enemy of our relationships with our children, our parents, and the church. It is his intention to distract and defeat us as often as he can without being spotted in the process. The apostle Peter reminds us to:

> Be of sober spirit, be on the alert. Your adversary, the devil, prowls about like a roaring lion, seeking someone to devour. But resist him, firm in your faith, knowing that the same experiences of suffering are being accomplished by your brethren who are in the world. And after you have suffered for a little while, the God of all grace, who called you to His eternal glory in Christ, will Himself perfect, confirm, strengthen and establish you (1 Peter 5:8-10).

As in the case with Job, there are times when the devil and his minions are allowed to come after us. God knows when that is happening, and God is always in charge. We need not fear the devil, for he has already been defeated by the power of Christ's death and resurrection. But misery loves company, and so the devil does what he can to sidetrack those who have fixed their hope on Christ. That's why Peter said we should be sober of spirit and on the alert.

Understanding Pain

In the story *The Velveteen Rabbit*, all the toys in the nursery wanted to be real. As a relative newcomer, the velveteen rabbit was not sure what it meant to be real, so he decided to ask the skin horse, who had been around for quite some time and who seemed very wise.

> "What is real?" asked the Rabbit one day, when they were lying side by side in the nursery. "Does it mean having things that buzz inside you and a stick-out handle?"
>
> "Real isn't how you are made," said the Skin Horse. "It's a thing that happens to you. When a child loves you for a long, long time, not just to play with, but REALLY loves you, then you become Real."
>
> "Does it hurt?" asked the Rabbit.
>
> "Sometimes," said the Skin Horse, for he was always truthful. "When you are Real, you don't mind being hurt."
>
> "Does it happen all at once, like being wound up," he asked, "or bit by bit?"
>
> "It doesn't happen all at once," said the Skin Horse. "You become. It takes a long time. That's why it doesn't often happen to people who break easily, or have sharp edges, or who have to be carefully kept. Generally, by the time you are Real, most of your hair has been loved off, and

> your eyes drop out and you get loose in the joints and
> very shabby. But these things don't matter at all, because
> once you are Real you can't be ugly, except to people
> who don't understand."
>
> MARGERY WILLIAMS BIANCO, *THE VELVETEEN RABBIT*, (NEW YORK, NY: SMITHMARK PUB.)

Your life and mine are significant simply because we are loved by God. He is in the business of making us real by loving us.

The way we react to pain and suffering will determine whether life's most tragic experiences bring us bitterness and despair or opportunities for growth and blessing. As Dorothy Sayers has written:

> Christianity has an enormous advantage over every
> other religion in the world. It is the *only* religion which
> gives value to evil and suffering. It affirms—not, like
> Christian Science, that evil has no real existence, nor yet,
> like Buddhism, that good consists in a refusal to experi-
> ence evil—but that perfection is attained through the
> active and positive effort to wrench a real good out of a
> real evil.[14]

Whatever pain or suffering you may be experiencing or have experienced, you can trust that God, in His divine purposes, has allowed it for your greatest good. He doesn't ask you to understand it fully; you only need to trust Him in the same way that one might expect earthly children to trust their loving parents. And as we place our confidence in God, trusting Him fully, the peace of God which goes beyond our comprehension is promised to be ours and we, like the velveteen rabbit, take another step closer to becoming real.

- Exactly what is faith?
- How would you define Christian faith?
- What exactly do Christians believe?
- How does Christian faith compare to other kinds of faith?
- What is a Christian, and where did the term "Christian" come from?
- How can Christian faith be relevant in our lives?

9

What Is Christian Faith?

It is...startling to discover how many people there are who heartily dislike and despise Christianity without having the faintest notion what it is. If you tell them, they cannot believe you....They simply cannot believe that anything so interesting, so exciting, and so dramatic can be the orthodox creed of the church.[15]

—*Dorothy Sayers*

Ya Gotta Have Faith

There's a story, and it may be an urban legend, that a certain bishop from a century ago pronounced from his pulpit that heavier-than-air flight was both impossible and contrary to the will of God.

The irony is that Bishop Wright had two sons, Orville and Wilbur.

Confident assertion does not define faith.

A bar in a small college town once displayed an interesting message on its marquee. It was parents' weekend and the bar owners were hoping to take advantage of the increased traffic, so they put up this message: "Bring your parents here for lunch, and we'll pretend we *don't* know you!"

Not wanting to be left out, the pastor of a clever little Baptist church just down the street from the bar also saw an opportunity. On their marquee he posted: "Bring your parents here for church on Sunday, and we'll pretend we *do* know you!"

But then, who you hang out with does not define faith either.

So What Is Faith?

Everybody on the planet has at least this much in common: We all believe in something. Even people who say, "I don't believe in anything!" believe that their statement of disbelief is true. It's simply impossible to live as a human being without having some kind of faith.

So what does the term "faith" mean? Our English word "faith" has its origins in the ancient Greek word *pistis* and the Latin *fides*. Both words indicate an inner attitude of confidence which results in a trusting relationship between human persons and God. Therefore, in defining faith, we should include at least two primary aspects: the intellectual aspect and the existential one. In other words, having faith includes first, believing that something or other is true. Then second, faith means having some kind of ensuing experience or relationship with the truth that is believed. You might say they are two wings of the same airplane, and the plane won't leave the ground without both. Christian faith has tangible, clearly defined, intellectual content and yet it is also practical, functional, experiential, and livable.

For example, if I believe that a certain chair can hold me (the intellectual aspect), and then I proceed to plop myself down in the chair (the existential aspect), I have passed through both aspects of having faith in the chair. First I came to the conclusion that the chair could hold my full weight, then trusting my conclusion, I sat down in the chair. And you will notice this is more than just agreeing with a propositional statement like "this chair can hold a person's full weight." I've gone beyond that by actually sitting down in the chair myself, demonstrating my confidence in the chair.

The Christian faith includes both these aspects. It's a faith that brings to the mind information and to the heart transformation. It's about both believing and embracing, understanding and standing in wide-eyed wonder. Both aspects of faith are essential. Without the intellectual side, faith becomes romantic wishful thinking, floppy and foggy, lacking in substance, difficult to count on when feelings and moods are running in another direction. But without the existential side, without a trusting relationship with the living God, faith is reduced to cold hard facts—lifeless data that fails to give courage to the heart, strength to the soul, and fire to the spirit.

What Is a Christian?

When asked what defines a Christian, many people might respond by saying a Christian is someone who "believes in God." While it's true that Christians do believe in God, that's not all there is to Christian faith. Acknowledging the existence of God is just the beginning of the intellectual half of Christian faith. It starts with the statement "God exists" but it doesn't end there. We must remember that, as the apostle James wrote, the demons believe God exists, too. (And I doubt anyone would suggest that the demons are Christians.)

Others think that if you are born into a Christian family then you are a Christian simply by default. But being a Christian is not defined by your relationship with your family. No one is a Christian simply because Mom, Dad, Gram, Gramps, and Uncle Eddie are all Christians. And while parents can have a profound impact on a child by training that child in the ways of Christian faith, if the child is ever actually to become a Christian, he or she must at some point come to a personal faith.

Likewise, being a Christian is not a function of what country, region, or state a person lives in. I love living in the South and I like Southerners quite a bit, but just because a person lives in the "Bible Belt" does not mean he or she is a Christian.

There are also those who think that being a Christian just means that you go to church on Sunday mornings. That's an interesting bit of logic, but if where you put your body on Sunday mornings is the determining factor, does that mean someone who goes to McDonald's on Sunday mornings is a Big Mac?

So, what is the difference?

When people who are Christians say, "I have faith in God," they don't just mean they acknowledge the existence of God. It is not truly Christian faith until there is also relationship between them and God. Just as when I put my confidence in the chair and sit down in it, if I am to have a real faith in God it must include the existential aspect, some way in which I begin to trust God with my life.

In keeping with the original meaning of faith, perhaps a more clear statement of faith in God would be something like, "I have confidence in God" or "I place my trust in God." Here we would be a little closer to the mark. It's at this point we finally are starting to get to the heart of what being a Christian is really all about.

Going Back to the Beginning

There's no better way to gain insight into what defines a true Christian than to go back to the beginning, to the time and place of the first people who were called "Christians." If anyone has the right to offer an authoritative definition for the term "Christian," it would be those who were there from the start.

As far as we know, "Christian" was originally coined by someone in the first century city of Antioch who was searching for a way to describe the followers of Jesus Christ. Antioch was the capital of Syria and the third largest city in the Greco-Roman Empire, surpassed in population only by Rome and Alexandria. Antioch could be compared to a modern-day city like New York or Los Angeles in that it was a huge melting pot of cultures, religions, and ethnicity. It was a city teeming with life, full of business opportunities, and open to all kinds of new ideas. As such, Antioch was a natural place for the newly born Christian faith to take root and begin to emerge.

Up until that time, most of the disciples of Jesus had come from Israel and were Jews. But since not all Jews had come to believe in Jesus, His followers could not rightly be identified just as "Jews." The population of greater Antioch was comprised of both Gentiles and Jews alike. As many people from both groups began converting to Christianity, the problem with how to identify them became complicated. They were Jews and Gentiles, yet they were no longer the same as other Jews and Gentiles. They had now pledged their allegiance to Jesus Christ, and yet they were without a proper name.

Then one day someone came up with the brilliant idea to call them by the name of the person they claimed to be following. And so, in a very natural way, these Gentile and Jewish believers in Jesus Christ became known as "Christians." A Christian then, in the original sense of the word, is someone who is following Jesus. Not in the sense of physical proximity from point A to point B, but in the sense that a Christian is someone who has placed his or her confidence in Christ as Lord.

Defined by What They Believed

As the early church grew, their leaders didn't try to reserve the message of the gospel for an elite group of enlightened Jewish disciples. They took Jesus' words to heart when He said:

> Go therefore and make disciples of all the nations, bap-
> tizing them in the name of the Father and the Son and
> the Holy Spirit, teaching them to observe all that I com-
> manded you; and lo, I am with you always, even to the
> end of the age (Matthew 28:19-20).

But just because you wear the jersey doesn't mean you are on
the team. People have a tendency to jump on bandwagons, so as
thousands of new people were being added to the church, it
became necessary to, as Jesus said, "teach them to observe all
that I commanded you." This teaching preserved the integrity of
the term "Christian," and whenever new converts were baptized,
a central aspect of their baptismal ceremony became making a
public declaration of precisely what it was they had come to
believe.

Over the first few centuries of the Christian church, several
creeds—or statements of faith—surfaced and were used to
summarize what people calling themselves Christians should
believe. The oldest and one of the most widely accepted creeds
is called the Apostle's Creed. It dates back to the second century
and has been embraced by Catholics, Anglicans, and Protestants
alike. If one creed could be said to exemplify the basic beliefs of
all Christians, it would certainly be the Apostle's Creed.

Familiarity can sometimes lead to obscurity. And since the
Apostle's Creed is so widely read and so often confessed, for
some it may have lost the impact of its meaning. Others may
find its formality and religious terminology unapproachable.
Still, to gain an understanding of the Christian faith, it will help
us to step outside of our own century and take a fresh look at
the depth and beauty found in this ancient statement of faith.

The Apostle's Creed

> I believe in God, the Father Almighty
> Maker of heaven and earth
> I believe in Jesus Christ, His only Son, our Lord.

He was conceived by the power of the Holy Spirit
And born of the virgin Mary.
He suffered under Pontius Pilate,
Was crucified, died and was buried.
On the third day He rose again.
He ascended into heaven
And is seated at the right hand of the Father.
He will come again to judge the living and
  the dead.
I believe in the Holy Spirit,
The holy catholic church,
The communion of saints,
The forgiveness of sins,
The resurrection of the body,
And the life everlasting.
Amen.

In general, the Apostle's Creed suggests that the Christian faith has at least three elements to it:

- The Christian faith has an object.

- The Christian faith has content.

- The Christian faith has function.

The *object* of the Christian faith is the Triune God of the Bible—God the Father, God the Son, and God the Holy Spirit. This Trinitarian view of God means that Christians believe that while God is one in essence, He is three in personality.

This may sound like a contradiction at first, but it really is not. A contradiction would be if we were to say that God is one in essence and at the same time claim that God is three in essence. However, God can be a unity in one way and a diversity in another. The unity of the God of the Bible is a unity of *essence*. The diversity of the God of the Bible is a diversity of *personality*.

Analogies all break down at some point, but one that sometimes helps people understand the Trinity is comparing God to the chemical substance H_2O. We know it in its liquid form as water, its vapor form as steam, and its solid form as ice. Water, steam, and ice are all one in essence (H_2O), but their appearance and function are different. It is similar with the Trinity of God the Father, God the Son, and God the Holy Spirit.

Many people have thought of God the Father as the transcendent aspect of God's personality, the one to whom we relate with reverence, awe, and wonder. God the Son has been seen as the more tangible personality, that part of the godhead who has drawn close and called us "friend" (John 15:13-15) and given us an example to follow. God the Spirit has been the more mysterious personality of the godhead but is quite active in all aspects of our relationship with God. The Spirit draws us close, lives within our hearts, empowers us to follow Christ, emboldens us to share His love with others, and encourages us toward growth and personal holiness.

The fact that we have some difficulty understanding what it means for God to be one in essence and three in personality simply shows that we are finite creatures trying to understand the infinite Creator. That's why the Trinity, the Virgin Birth, the Incarnation, and other elements of our faith can be classified as *mystery*. This is one of the reasons Jesus said we would have to become as children to enter the kingdom of heaven. Children can embrace mystery much easier than adults. Adults tend to become too jaded, too self sufficient, and too used to being able to figure it all out. Hence our struggle with the mysteries of Christianity.

The *content* of the Christian faith is found in the creed's factual statements. These statements all have their origin in the pages of the Bible, and they show us that there are definable and knowable things about God, about humanity, and about the relationship that can exist between the two. While we can't know *everything* about God, we can know *something* about God.

The *function* of the Christian faith is the existential aspect of faith and can be seen in the last several lines of this poetic statement of faith. It describes experiences and relationships that stem from our Christian belief both as individuals and corporately as members of the body of Christ. *Church, communion, forgiveness, resurrection,* and *life everlasting*—these all deal with the function of our faith and the way it is lived out in the community of believers and as a testimony to nonbelievers.

A Closer Look at the Creed

Taking a closer look at the Apostle's Creed unfolds a wealth of information about Christian faith. Within the creed we discover that the Christian faith is overflowing with things to know, things to experience, and things to do.

The Apostle's Creed begins where it should, with God.

I believe in God, the Father Almighty

This first line gives rise to some fascinating insights. Notice the choice and positioning of the two terms "Father" and "Almighty." Most of us would think of these as almost opposite terms, and yet they're placed right next to each other. How could someone as unfathomable as the Almighty God be as personal as anyone's father? Yet the creed tells us that the God of the universe is indeed both approachable *and* awesome. God is intimate enough to love us like a father, yet powerful enough to save us like only the Almighty can. God is imminent *and* transcendent, personal *and* infinite. Knowing this about God provides a unique hope for anyone searching for a meaningful relationship with Him.

Maker of heaven and earth

"Maker of heaven and earth" offers us insight into that great cosmological question: "Where did everything come from?"

With all the beauty and order seen throughout the physical universe, with such clear evidence of intelligent design, the Christian faith corresponds with reality and proclaims, "Yes! It was designed. The designer is God, and you can know God as your heavenly Father!"

The natural world has come into being because God created it. God Himself is not a part of creation; He is its Creator. God is not merely the energy the universe runs on, but rather He sustains the universe by His own power. God stands behind everything that exists. He is the author of reason, the juggler of stars, and the composer of the nightingale's song. He taught the spider how to spin her web and the dog how to be faithful. God also generously created you and me in His own image with a hunger to know Him.

Next the creed tells us the amazing story of how God made it possible for us to come into a relationship with Him. This section speaks about the person who stands at the center of Christian faith, our Lord and Savior Jesus Christ, the very Son of God.

**I believe in Jesus Christ, His only Son, our Lord.
He was conceived by the power of the Holy Spirit
And born of the virgin Mary.**

When some people think of Christianity, they think of it as a list of moral rules, a bunch of dos and don'ts too numerous to count and too strict for anyone to ever live up to. For many it boils down to never having a good time, avoiding sex, beer, and cigarettes, and making sure that you are at the church building every time the doors are unlocked. The blame for this complete misunderstanding of Christianity falls squarely at our feet as Christians. We have been guilty of foisting such thinking on people for the past two centuries, and it's high time we invite people to lean in and take a closer look, to discover that true Christianity is really quite different from all that.

At the center of the Christian faith stands a poor Jewish carpenter turned rabbi, hardly the respectable type, who came from Nazareth, a town which in His time would have been considered as "the *other* side of the tracks." He traveled around speaking in parables, proverbs, and paradoxes, embracing outcasts and outsiders, touching and healing even the most needy of the sick and maimed. He became a friend to tax collectors, prostitutes, and misfits. The religious leaders of His day called Him a "glutton and wine bibber, a friend of sinners." To them He responded by blasting their hypocrisy and external religiosity. To those who would believe, He became their loving Lord and Savior.

In the creed you can't help but notice the unique conception of Christ by the Holy Spirit and then His birth to a young Jewish peasant girl who was still a virgin. "Incarnation" is the term we use to describe how God became one of us, how the Creator of the entire universe condescended to become a part of His creation. It's like a painter stepping into and becoming a part of his or her own painting. And how incredible that God chose Mary to mother the Christ. Why not choose a wealthy aristocrat's daughter? Why not an esteemed military man's daughter? How about a princess or someone with some other lofty credentials?

The answer is simple: Because the gospel is for anyone who will believe, whether rich or poor, intellectual or imbecile. No matter who you are, Christ has come to rescue you if you will simply place your trust in Him.

The New Testament tells us that Jesus went around claiming to be one with God and that anyone who had seen Him had seen God the Father. This wouldn't have been significant if Christ had been a pantheist, but He was a Jew. This made His claim of deity completely outrageous. The idea that Jesus Christ was both God and man is hard to comprehend, but it makes so much sense when you think about it. To accomplish the task of being our Savior, Jesus had to be both. If Jesus were God and nothing else, He could not have represented us and died in our place for our sins. Had Jesus been just a man, His death would mean nothing more than yours or mine.

He suffered under Pontius Pilate,
Was crucified, died and was buried.
On the third day He rose again.
He ascended into heaven
And is seated at the right hand of the Father.
He will come again to judge the living and the dead.

One of the reasons I believe Christianity to be true is that it rests on a solid foundation of verifiable, historical credibility. It is not a mere fantasy or fairy tale. Jesus was a real person living in the real world. The mention of Pontius Pilate in the creed sets the life and ministry of Christ in the context of recorded history. Pilate was the procurator of Judea who served under the Roman emperor Tiberias Caesar.

That Jesus was crucified, died, and was buried leaves no question about the mission of Christ. He came to die for our sins. This He did of His own volition, even though He was executed by the Romans at the request of the Jewish religious leaders. This was God's plan all along, and Jesus carried it out with foresight and precision.

That Jesus rose again on the third day is a grand display of the victory of the cross wherein Christ defeated the power of death. Since Jesus was both God and man, His death means that when the human person Jesus died, God the Son died too. Likewise, when God the Son rose from the grave, the human person Jesus did as well.

While the *fact* of the resurrection confirms and establishes the identity of Christ, the *significance* of the resurrection does something else. It's not just about the ten minutes or the ten days after the stone was rolled away. But because Christ was victorious over death, He did what no person had ever done before. He literally dismantled death. He took it apart and left it lying in broken pieces on the floor of the heavenly realm.

Jesus then ascended into heaven where He is seated at the right hand of the Father. And if there is still a question in anyone's mind about His divinity, the fact that He will come again to judge the living and the dead clearly shows that Jesus has an authority that only God could possibly claim.

I believe in the Holy Spirit

The Scriptures tell us that the Holy Spirit has been active since the very beginning of creation (Genesis 1:2). Throughout the Bible we see examples of the Holy Spirit's multifaceted ministry of working in the lives of individuals and entire nations. Since the time of Christ, the Spirit's ministry can be summarized by saying that the Holy Spirit:

- Convinces us of the truth (John 16:13).

- Convicts us of our sin (John 16:8).

- Converts us into new creatures (Titus 3:5).

- Connects us to the Body of Christ (1 Corinthians 12:13).

- Comforts us in our trials (Acts 9:31).

- Conforms us into the image of Christ (1 Peter 1:2).

The mention of the Holy Spirit at the beginning of this last section of the creed at least suggests the role He plays in all that follows. It's the work of the Holy Spirit that makes us members of the universal church as He baptizes us into the body of Christ (1 Corinthians 12:13). It's the Spirit's ministry that fills us with the love of God and enables us to commune with each other

(Romans 5:5). And it is the Spirit who is the voice of our conscience and convicts us of sin and leads us to repentance whereupon we receive the forgiveness of our sins (John 16:8).

The holy catholic church

The word "church" comes from the Greek word *ekklesia*, which refers to a group of people who have been "called out" or "separated" from the rest of the world. Unlike the common concept and usage of the word, the church mentioned in the creed does not refer to a building made of red bricks, white trim, and a steeple. Those who belong to the church have been called out of the kingdom of this world into the kingdom of God and as such, they are members with each other of what is called the "body of Christ."

The adjective "catholic" in the creed comes from the Greek word *katholikos,* which means "according to the whole" and refers to the universal nature of the church. Some have erroneously thought it refers specifically to the Roman Catholic Church. But since the creed was being used some 850 years before the formation of the distinct, institutionalized Roman Catholic Church, this is not so. All those who place their trust in Christ for salvation are members of the universal church. Whether you go to a building with a sign bearing the name Catholic, Baptist, Calvary Chapel, Presbyterian, Methodist, or something else, if you have placed your trust in Christ, you are a part of His universal church.

Those who have leveled complaints against Christianity usually point to some discrepancy between what the Christian faith teaches and how well it is lived out by members of the church. And the fact is, if we were to be honest about it, we'd have to admit that we Christians do and say some pretty dumb things at times. That said, I want you to know that really that's the point of the whole thing anyway, isn't it? The reason we need Christ in the first place is because there really is something wrong with us, and we stand in desperate need of the kind of transformation of heart and mind that only the Spirit of God can bring to us. As far as I have seen, that transformation doesn't come all at once. It comes in steps—sometimes little baby steps. But it is fostered and nurtured through the mutual encouragement and accountability that can be found within the church.

Someone will say, "But the church is full of hypocrites!" And again we must admit it. The church *is* full of hypocrites. But the world is full of hypocrites too, because basically *all* people are hypocrites, and for some reason Christ has chosen to populate the church with people instead of aardvarks.

Hypocrisy is exhausting, especially when it's your own. But as Christians, we can take comfort in knowing that while we aren't what we should be, by God's grace we also aren't what we used to be either. And as we go through the process of living out our faith in the community of believers, we can truly learn and grow.

If I were to make one observation about a serious weakness I see in the church, it would be that we have exchanged the depth of *being* the church for the shallowness of just *going* to church. Somewhere we lost sight of our focus and function. The writer of Hebrews put it this way: "Let us consider how to stimulate one another to love and good deeds, not forsaking our own assembling together, as is the habit of some, but encouraging one another; and all the more as you see the day drawing near" (Hebrews 10:24-25). His point was not mandatory attendance every time the doors are unlocked, but that when we assemble, it is for a reason. And it's not to pat ourselves on the back with attendance pins, show off our new Easter dress or Armani suit or BMW. The church is supposed to be a place where we are mutually enriched in spite of our individual spiritual poverty.

The communion of saints

We are to be participants in the body of Christ, not just observers. None of us is a spiritual island. We need the stimulation of others to move us toward love and good deeds. We need the encouragement of others who are struggling with the same issues we are struggling with. And even if you don't think you need *them*, according to the Bible, they need *you*.

Don't allow conceit, laziness, or intellectual snobbery to keep you from participating in the communion of the saints. Or if you wrestle with being a part of the church from the opposite side, don't allow feelings of intimidation, inadequacy, and insecurity keep you from meeting regularly with others who, in their honest moments, would have to admit to the same struggles. The point is we need each other if we are to grow. As Proverbs 27:17 says: "Iron sharpens iron, so one man sharpens another."

The church is a place where Christians can *belong*. Christians are mystically united with each other in a spiritual bond which runs across national, ethnic, racial, gender, and age barriers, and so for Christians all secondary distinctions do not really matter. If you love Christ, you are my brother or my sister; we are spiritual siblings in the family of God, and we should come together to share our burdens and our blessings, the discouragements and encouragements of our journey toward maturity in Christ.

The forgiveness of sins

This line of the creed acknowledges at least two things. First, that there are such things as sins and second, that these sins can be forgiven.

To many people, sin is just a religious-sounding word that has lost its meaning. But ever since the beginning, sin has referred to the deliberate violation of the will of God and is attributable to our arrogance, self-centeredness, and rebellion. The effect of sin is that it causes separation. It separates us from

God, from others, and even from our true selves. Foolishly following our passions like a dog follows its nose, we put our own interests first, our own desires over the desires of others, and basically we do what we want, when we want to.

The word "sin" has a dual meaning throughout Scripture. It is used in both a legal and a personal sense. In the legal sense it refers to the condition of original sin, or the fact that all of us, as descendants of the first sinners, have been born with a sinful nature and are therefore guilty before God. All of us have a sinful nature. Anyone who has ever been around a sweet and cuddly little baby knows that in spite of how cute the little darling may be, no one has to teach him or her how to be selfish. As G.K. Chesterton observed, original sin is one of the easiest doctrines of the Christian faith to prove simply because you can see it at work all around us.

In the personal sense, the term "sin" refers to my acts of sin and your acts of sin. Because we are born with a sinful nature, not only are we guilty before God, but we are also spiritually polluted. This pollution causes us to think and behave in ways that are contrary to the will of God. Instead of being "God-centered" or "other-centered," we go about our lives "self-centered." Our motto tends to be: "I want what I want, and I want it now!" Even though we may never say it aloud, we live out our lives with what is, in effect, a moral wink and nod, readily excusing ourselves for what we would quickly condemn in others. Because of our spiritual pollution, we are unable to see life clearly, and we are even unable to see ourselves clearly.

This is where the beautiful promise of God's grace comes in. When we accept Christ as our Savior, the Bible tells us that we are justified by faith, which means our sin is forgiven by God. And then, as we confess our individual acts of sin, God deals with the pollution in our hearts by cleansing us from these specific personal sins. Because of the complete and finished work of

Christ in His death on the cross, forgiveness is available to us in both the legal and the personal sense.

The Bible's concepts of grace and forgiveness are two of the major teachings of the Christian faith that make it stand out from all other religions. By God's grace, salvation and forgiveness are made available to us. We can't pay for this gift ourselves. We can't earn it by working harder to be good, by sinning less often, by going to church more, by reading our Bible more, or by praying for hours on end. It's simply offered to us for free. That's why it is called *amazing grace*.

This is pretty hard for us to fathom. We tend to think that when someone offers us anything for free, there must be something wrong with it, there must be some hidden hook or some scam behind it. But that isn't the case with God's forgiveness. It is offered to us for free because Christ died on the cross and paid the price for our sin.

How do we take advantage of this free gift of God? The apostle John tells us, "If we confess our sins, He [God] is faithful and righteous to forgive us our sins and to cleanse us from all unrighteousness" (1 John 1:9).

What is our part? We must acknowledge our sin, confessing it to God. This requires humility, the convicting work of the Holy Spirit, and some honest soul-searching. But as long as we are aware of our sin, matters are not completely hopeless. Dissatisfaction with ourselves in this regard is the sign of a healthy conscience. The time to worry is when we get to the point of thinking we are not sinners.

What is God's part? That same verse from 1 John says that God is faithful to forgive us and cleanse us. That means our hearts are washed from the stain and pollution of our sin. That means we are made new and the slate is wiped clean. If you have been struggling with a burden of guilt for some past sin, take a moment right now and pray to God, confessing and acknowledging what you have done as sin, and then ask God to set you free with His gracious gift of forgiveness through Christ. You can trust God to do His part. He has had plenty of practice with forgiveness. After all, He invented it.

The resurrection of the body, And the life everlasting.

The Apostle's Creed ends by answering one of the greatest questions that has ever haunted the human heart: Is this life all there is?

The creed and the Christian faith say, "No!" Physical death is not the end.

We all experience a longing that nothing in this life ever quite seems to satisfy. As St. Augustine has said, "You (God) have made us for yourself and our hearts will be restless until we find our rest in you." When will we realize that the deepest longing of our hearts is not for celebrity, more money, bigger houses, nicer cars, better spouses, or anything that can be charged to a credit card? What we all long for, what our souls really yearn for, is a connection with our Creator, a relationship with the Father Almighty. And, as the creed says, those who have had their sins forgiven and come into a relationship with God through Christ, have God's assurance that this life is not all there is.

There will come a day when God brings history to a close. Part of that final sequence of events includes the resurrection of the dead. Those who have placed their confidence in Christ will be raised to the joy of life everlasting in the presence of God.

Making the Creed Personal

In just over 100 words the Apostle's Creed spells out the basics of the Christian faith. It shows us that Christianity is not some vague, foggy, or shapeless spirituality. Nor is it a simplistic, shallow, romantic spirituality. Its essence does not consist of a legalistic set of rules and regulations. At its core, Christianity is not so much a religion as it is a vital relationship with the living God.

If you really desire to understand the Christian faith it must be from the inside. You must come to know God as *your* Father Almighty by acknowledging Jesus as *your* Lord. Then the Holy Spirit will transform your life and fill your heart with the peace of God.

10

When God Asked Questions

God comes to us, not only to give us peace,
but also to disturb us. Inner restlessness and
disquiet can well be God sowing the first
seeds of faith in the human heart.

—*John Powell*

Letting Fair Be Fair

If turnabout is fair play—and I have spent most of my words
dealing with the questions we ask about God—then perhaps it
would be appropriate to close out this book by looking at a
question or two God has asked us.

It may seem odd to think of God asking us questions. What
doesn't the Almighty already know? What have we learned so
much about that we have now surpassed the all-knowing, infinite one? In what subject does God need us to inform Him? Is
He somehow curious about our adventures into outer space,
quantum physics, computer science, or genetic engineering?

The fact is, questions are not only asked by the uninformed. Sometimes they are asked by the informed to help the uninformed become informed. For centuries teachers and communicators have used rhetorical questions to emphasize, clarify, and embellish ideas which can sometimes be difficult to understand. And these rhetoricians have simply been copying what God did from the very beginning—ask questions to make a point.

Questions from God the Father

What questions does God ask us? What are the purposes of God's questions?

It began early on, right after Adam and Eve were drawn in by the question posed by that sneaky serpent in the garden: "Indeed, has God said, 'You shall not eat from any tree of the garden?'" (Genesis 3:1). Probably to their ears it sounded more like this: "Oh come on! Who is God to be cramping *your* freedom?"

The fruit looked so good and the idea of being as smart as God certainly sounded great. It was too much to resist. They ate and waited for the magic to happen. Nothing. They took another bite and waited some more. Nothing. Maybe one of them thought: "Must be a timed release thing that will hit us later." Truer words were never spoken.

Sometime later, when they heard the footsteps of God as He came to meet with them in the garden, it did finally hit them. They felt something they'd never felt before, and it didn't feel good at all. They felt shame...that painful emotion caused by the awareness of real, deserved guilt, a recognition of their shortcomings, impropriety, and embarrassment. So Adam and Eve ran out into the forest and tried to hide themselves from God's presence.

What must that experience have been like for God? What was going on in the heart and mind of God as His nearest and dearest creatures were now scrambling to get away from Him? He had given them the run of the place and the freedom to do just about anything. All their needs were met. They didn't have to work, didn't have to pay taxes, and didn't need health insurance because they wouldn't be getting sick. God had given the man and woman charge over everything; He had given them all those great pets to take care of and to play with. He had even given Adam and Eve to each other for love, companionship, and pleasure. They could live without any cares, enjoying life to the fullest.

There was only one house rule and it was actually for their benefit. The existence of the rule gave them real moral significance. Respecting it would keep them from being eternally separated from God. With all He had given them, how could they have disregarded this one little restriction?

Perhaps it is presumptuous for us to speculate on this. We can't really know exactly how God felt. We can only imagine how we would have felt, standing in that beautifully lit garden now stained with the first shadows of darkness. But God knew that for Adam and Eve to be morally significant, He had to offer them the real opportunity to choose to disobey Him. And sure enough, they did.

It was then that the Almighty, the all-knowing God of the universe, asked His very first question: "Where are you?"

God wasn't in the dark here. They were. Darkness runs in fear from even the least bit of light, and here, with the approaching light of God's presence, the darkness of shame led to the deeper darkness of fear, which led to the deepest darkness of all, separation from God.

Adam heard God's question and said, "I heard the sound of Thee in the garden, and I was afraid because I was naked; and I hid myself" (Genesis 3:10 RSV).

For the first time in the mind of any human, God was thought of as someone to be feared. Not in a respectful sense, but in the sense of being someone to run from. How horrible that must have been for God. How it must have grieved Him that the two He made in His own image had chosen to bring on this separation and now thought of Him as someone to avoid at all costs.

It was clear that they knew on an instinctual level what had happened—that's why they hid themselves, that's why they were afraid. But since God had created them as thinking people too, He asked the question, hoping they would connect the dots between their shame and its cause.

As any loving parent knows, when you are trying to teach a moral lesson to a child who has messed up, it requires communicating a full understanding of what was expected and how those expectations were not met. Character does not improve in the vacuum of acquiescence. Love does not mean just letting things slide all the time. Sometimes love must be tough enough to confront the realities of fallen nature. That doesn't make it easy on a parent who has a difficult child, and that didn't make it easy on God.

And so once again, for the second and third time in the history of the universe, God asked questions.

"And He [God] said, 'Who told you that you were naked? Have you eaten from the tree of which I commanded you not to eat?'" (Genesis 3:11).

Both questions pointed something out to our ancestral parents. In essence God said to them: "What was the source of this shame and fear you now feel? Did you listen to another voice? Did you willfully disobey me?" How patient of God. How generous to take the time to educate and inform, to help Adam and Eve understand where they had gone wrong and why they were feeling the way they felt.

By their sin, Adam and Eve opened the door that let the darkness in, and all of humanity has been living in the shadows ever since. But even in those early days of human history, God had already set in motion a plan to restore our relationship with Him. Throughout the Bible we see humankind's needs being met by the gracious, loving God. Over and over again, we see God transforming our humiliating disgrace with His amazing grace.

The Lord is still interested in an answer to that first question: "Where are you?" It should make us stop and take note of any separation that has come between us and God. It's a good question to consider. Where are you spiritually? What is the condition of your spiritual life? Do you find yourself in full fellowship with God? Or are you running and hiding whenever you hear His footsteps?

Questions from God the Son

When Jesus came to earth there were questions on His lips as well. One of them, which He asked more than once, was simply this: "Who do you say that I am?" He asked it of the religious leaders of His day, He asked it of His disciples, and He asked it of the multitudes.

This one question cuts to the center of the Christian faith because, ultimately, the Chritian faith is not a religion. It's not about a code of conduct or trying to balance the moral scales by doing more good things than bad. Ultimately, the Christain faith is about our response to what Christ has done for us, the fact that He died on the cross to pay for our sins and make it possible for us to step out of the darkness and back into the light.

Where are you? and Who do you say that I am?

"Where are you?" and "Who do you say that I am?" The answer to the second question is the secret to dealing with the problem we encouter in the first.

With the first question the Bible tells us that all of us are sinners and are therefore separated from God. Where are we? We are hiding from God. We are all spiritually in the dark. It is as if we are trapped in a dark room behind a locked door. We can see that there is light on the other side of the door but we do not have the key. We sense that God is there but we realize we are removed from any personal relationship with Him.

In the person of Jesus Christ, God has come and unlocked the door for us. He even swings the door open and calls for us to come out of the darkness and into the light. When we hear His call and we answer the question, "Who do you say that I am?" by acknowledging that Jesus is the Christ, the One who died for our sin, *our* savior, then we accept Christ as the answer to our sin problem and Christ takes us from darkness and brings us into the light. No longer separated from God, we live in fullness and freedom in the light of His grace. The apostle Paul said it this way:

> For you were formerly darkness, but now you are light in the Lord; walk as children of the light (Ephesians 5:8).

"Where are you?" and "Who do you say that I am?" Your answer to these two important questions can mark the beginning of your life with God as a Christian. As you continue on your faith journey, to be sure, there will be many other questions that will cross your mind. But take them as they come and remember the life of faith is not so much a sprint as it is a marathon. Run with patience the race that is set before you, always looking to Jesus, who is the author and perfecter of your faith.

And as you come to know Him better, may the Lord give you a clearer vision of His truth, a greater faith in His power, and a more confident assurance of His love for you.

Untangling Basic Theological Terms

Agnostic—A person who believes that we cannot ultimately know the answers to our questions about spiritual issues.

Anthropomorphism—Attributing human characteristics or actions (e.g. eyes, seeing, ears, hearing, etc.) to something non-human such as God, angels, or the devil.

Apostle—An apostle is one sent on a mission. In the case of the Christian apostles, this term refers to those whom Jesus personally selected to represent Him, establish the church, and define Christian doctrine. They were eyewitnesses to the fact that Jesus had been raised from the dead, and they were charged with the mission of spreading the good news of the gospel to the world at large. There were 12 apostles appointed by Jesus from among the original disciples. After Judas betrayed Christ, he was replaced by Matthias. Paul, who had also seen the risen Christ in a vision on the road to Damascus, was also called an apostle.

Atheist—A person who denies the existence of God.

Atonement—The word means "to satisfy." As a theological term it refers to the action of Christ in reconciling mankind to God. By His death on the cross, Christ purchased our salvation and satisfied both the justice and mercy of God.

Baptism—A ceremony in which new converts to Christianity make a symbolic, public declaration of what has happened to them on a spiritual level. Baptism symbolizes the new believer's identification with Christ in both His death and resurrection. New believers declare their death to their former life and their resurrection to a new life in Christ.

Body of Christ—The analogy used by the apostle Paul to describe the mystical union of believers with Christ as our "head" and with each other as fellow members or parts of the body of Christ. It speaks of our diversity in that a body has many parts, and of our unity in that the body is still one.

Calling—A summons or directive from God, initially to turn from our sin and follow Christ, but also at times to specific works in the church or the world as servants of God.

Canon—The term used to denote the list of books generally accepted into the Bible as the authoritative Word of God. This list includes the 39 books of the Old Testament and the 27 books of the New Testament.

Catholic—Technically this term means "universal," as it's used in the Apostle's Creed. In contemporary usage it often refers to anything having to do with the Roman Catholic Church.

Confession—There are two ways in which this term can be used. First, it may describe the confession of sin in which a person acknowledges their wrong doing and their remorse for having displeased God. Second, it can mean to declare your faith in, adherence to, or agreement with a teaching. When we confess the Apostle's Creed we are declaring that we believe the statements of the creed to be true.

Consecration—The setting apart of people or things for the service of God.

Conversion—The combination of repentance and faith which leads someone to turn and follow Christ. The circumstances under which this happens are unique for every person who comes to follow Him.

Covenant—The agreement or promise offered by God which is designed to secure a relationship between God and humankind. Prior to Christ, God had offered the Old Covenant of the Law, which failed because of humanity's inability to live up to it. Now, through Christ, we have the New Covenant of Grace.

Creed—A summary of belief. The Christian church has adopted several, the most widely accepted of which are the Apostle's Creed and the Nicene Creed.

Cult—A group that is a deviation from true Christianity. Its followers usually display an intense loyalty to their leadership. These groups often take an unbalanced approach to interpreting Scripture, mutual accountability, and methods and forms of worship, twisting them or distorting them from their original and true meaning.

Deism—This is a term that is generally associated with a group of seventeenth-century English writers who propagated the idea that while God was responsible for the creation of the world, He is no longer involved in the affairs of His creation.

Doctrine—The body of principles which are given through teaching and instruction.

Epistemology—That branch of philosophy which deals with the origins, limits, and methods of human knowledge.

Epistle—Another term for *letters*, usually referring to the letters written by the various apostles and contained in the New Testament.

Eschatology—That part of theology which deals with the end times or last days, especially concerned with the Second Coming of Christ and the end of this present world.

Eternal life—Life without end, even when we leave this temporal world. Eternal life is the free gift of God for those who have placed their trust in Christ.

Evangelical—This term has evolved a good bit over the years but is used in a general way to refer to those who embrace the supreme authority of the Scripture as God's Word and the atoning death of Christ as the only means of salvation.

Evangelism—A term describing any effort to convince others of the truth of the gospel and to persuade them to become Christians.

Faith—In the Christian sense, faith means a belief and trust in God which results in a strong allegiance and loyalty to Him. The New Testament tells us that "faith is the assurance of things hoped for, the conviction of things not seen" (Hebrews 11:1).

Fall, the—The original event whereby humankind chose to willfully disobey God, which resulted in separation from God, the distortion of the image of God in humanity, the spoiling of the rest of creation, and the curse of death.

Filled with the Spirit—That ongoing experience of yielding ourselves completely to the Holy Spirit for enrichment, empowerment, and employment.

Gifts of the Spirit—The variety of special abilities given by the Holy Spirit to believers to be used for the good of the entire body of Christ. These are listed in Romans 12, 1 Corinthians 12, and Ephesians 4.

Gospel—The *good news* about how Jesus Christ has come to offer us forgiveness and eternal life through His death and resurrection. "The Gospels" refer to the first four books in the New Testament: Matthew, Mark, Luke, and John.

Grace—In Christian theology, grace is the unearned and undeserved gift of God whereby He offers forgiveness and salvation to sinners, and where God's influence works in us, giving us a new life in Christ. While *mercy* means "not getting what we deserve," grace means "getting something we do not deserve."

Heaven—The place where we are in the eternal presence of God and experience all the fullness of His love, joy, and peace, as well as the absence of the negative effects of the Fall (e.g., sickness, sorrow, death, etc.).

Heresy—Teaching that departs from and contradicts established, orthodox truth.

Hell—Also referred to as *Hades, Sheol,* and *Gehenna.* The place of eternal torment and separation from God.

Holy—Set apart for God and His service. We are called to be *holy* and to reflect the image of God in Christ.

Incarnation—The term which describes how God the Son took on flesh and became a man in the person of Jesus Christ. This doctrine teaches that Jesus Christ was both God and man at the same time, having both a divine and a human nature.

Inspiration—The means by which God communicated to the authors of the Bible precisely what He wanted included in His word.

Judgment—The action of God whereby He holds all people accountable for their thoughts and deeds. Both believers and unbelievers will face the final judgment of God. Believers will be declared "not guilty" because they have placed their trust in Christ and His work on the cross on their behalf.

Justification—A term which describes how a sinner is made acceptable to God as God moves that person from the status of guilty to not guilty by His grace. This is not arbitrary, but occurs when the repentant sinner places faith in Christ and His atoning work on the cross.

Law, the—This term usually refers to the Ten Commandments and/or the first five books of the Old Testament, in which God defines the patterns of behavior for His people to express their love for God and each other.

Messiah—The Hebrew term also referred to by its Greek version *Christ*. It is the title of the one God anointed to set His people free from their sin.

Mystery—That which is beyond human understanding and explanation.

Natural theology—The general knowledge of God arrived at through human reason alone and apart from any specific divine revelation.

Omnipotent—All powerful, able to do anything that can be done.

Omnipresent—Present everywhere at the same time.

Omniscient—All-knowing, all-wise.

Original sin—Our predisposition toward sinful thoughts and deeds.

Orthodox—Correct doctrine, true to the original idea, conforming to the established standards.

Pantheist—A person who believes that everything is an aspect of the divine. A pantheist might worship nature and believes in a kind of moral neutrality.

Polytheist—A person who believes in more than one god.

Protestant—A term referring to any member of a non-Catholic Christian church. The term comes from a sixteenth-century protest movement against Catholic doctrine and practices.

Providence—The care and guidance of God over all creation and specifically over those who have placed themselves under His care by trusting in Christ.

Redemption—The act of Christ in dying for our sins to purchase our salvation.

Reformed—An adjective which connotes ties to the teachings of the sixteenth-century reformer John Calvin.

Regeneration—The act of the Holy Spirit in which we are given a new birth to a new life in Christ.

Repentance—Having a change of mind and heart which leads to a change of behavior or attitude. Turning away from our sin and turning toward God.

Resurrection—The historical, space-time event where God raised Jesus from the dead and dismantled death forever. The significance of this event confirms the deity of Christ and offers those who place their trust in Christ assurance that this life is not the end.

Revelation—The initiative God takes to unfold or unveil information about Himself, His plans, and His purposes. Revelation makes knowledge available to us that we would otherwise have no access to, as it is simply beyond human reason and discovery. It is also the name of the last book in the New Testament.

Salvation—Also referred to as *redemption*, the act of God whereby He rescues the souls of repentant humans from the dire circumstances of punishment we are due because of our guilt and the pollution of our sin.

Sanctification—Following *justification*, sanctification is the ongoing process of renewal toward holiness in the life of the believer accomplished by the Holy Spirit.

Theism—Belief in God.

Theology—The study of God and God's relationships with humanity and all of creation.

Trinity—The unity of God in three persons known as God the Father, God the Son, and God the Holy Spirit. The Christian view holds that while God is one in essence, God is three in personality and function.

Bibliography

Adler, Mortimer J. *Truth in Religion.* New York: Collier Books, 1990.

Berkhof, Louis. *Systematic Theology.* Grand Rapids: Wm. B. Eerdmans Publishing Co., 1996.

Chesterton, G.K. *Orthodoxy.* New York: Image Books/Doubleday, 1959.

Clark, Kelly James. *Philosophers Who Believe.* Downers Grove: InterVarsity Press, 1993.

Erickson, Millard J. *Christian Theology.* Grand Rapids: Baker Books, 1998.

———. *Saved by Grace.* Grand Rapids: Wm. B. Eerdmans Publishing Co., 1989.

Lewis, C.S. *Mere Christianity.* New York: Macmillan Publishing, 1979.

———. *Miracles.* New York: The MacMillan Company, 1947.

———. *The Problem of Pain.* New York: Macmillan Publishing, 1962.

———. *The Screwtape Letters.* New York: The MacMillan Company, 1943.

———. *The Weight of Glory.* New York: Macmillan Publishing, 1980.

McDowell, Josh and Wilson, Bill. *The Best of Josh McDowell: A Ready Defense.* Nashville: Thomas Nelson, Inc., 1993.

McGrath, Alister E. *Historical Theology.* Malden: Blackwell Publishers Inc., 1998.

———. *I Believe: Exploring the Apostle's Creed.* Downers Grove: InterVarsity Press, 1997.

———. *Studies in Doctrine.* Grand Rapids: Zondervan Publishing House, 1997.

Moreland, J.P. and Nielsen, Kai. *Does God Exist?* Buffalo: Prometheus Books, 1993.

Nash, Ronald H. *Faith and Reason.* Grand Rapids: Zondervan, 1988.

Pascal, Blaise. *Pensées, The Provincial Letters.* New York: Random House, 1941.

Pinnock, Clark H. *Reason Enough.* Downers Grove: InterVarsity Press, 1980.

Plantinga, Alvin C. *God, Freedom, and Evil.* Grand Rapids: Wm. B. Eerdmans Publishing Co., 1986.

Sayers, Dorothy L. *Creed or Chaos?* London: Methuen & Co. Ltd., 1954.

Schaeffer, Francis A. *The God Who is There.* Downers Grove: InterVarsity Press, 1968.

———. *True Spirituality.* Wheaton: Tyndale House Publishers, 1971.

Sproul, R.C.; Gerstner, John and Lindsley, Arthur. *Classical Apologetics.* Grand Rapids: The Zondervan Company, 1984.

Sproul, R.C. *Not a Chance.* Grand Rapids: Baker Books, 1994.

Stott, John R.W. *The Authority of the Bible.* Downers Grove: InterVarsity Press, 1974.

———. *The Cross of Christ.* Downers Grove: InterVarsity Press, 1986.

Wells, David F. *God in the Wasteland.* Grand Rapids: Wm. B. Eerdmans Publishing Co., 1994.

Notes

1. Mortimer J. Adler, *Truth in Religion* (New York, NY: Collier Books/Macmillan, 1990), p. 21.

2. Blaise Pascal, *Pensées* 265.

3. Nancy R. Pearcey and Charles B. Thaxton, *The Soul of Science* (Wheaton, IL: Crossway Books, 1994), p. 222.

4. Josh McDowell and Don Stewart, *Answers to Tough Questions* (Wheaton, IL: Tyndale House, 1980).

5. John R.W. Stott, *The Authority of the Bible* (Downers Grove: InterVarsity Press, 1974).

6. C.S. Lewis, *God in the Dock* (Grand Rapids, MI: William B. Eerdmans Publishing, 1970), pp. 157-158.

7. Frederick Buechner, *Wishful Thinking* (HarperSanFrancisco, 1973), p. 20.

8. St. Augustine, *The Problem of Free Choice*, Vol. 22 of *Ancient Christian Writers* (Westminster, MD: The Newman Press, 1955), pp. 14-15.

9. C.S. Lewis, *The Problem of Pain* (New York, NY: Macmillan Publishing Company, 1962), p. 39.

10. Anthony A. Hoekema, *Created in God's Image* (Grand Rapids, MI: Wm. B. Eerdmans Publishing Co., 1986), pp. 136-138.

11. Dorothy Sayers, *Creed or Chaos?* (London: Methuen & Co. Ltd., 1954), p. 2.

12. See Jonah 1–4.

13. See Matthew 8:18-27.

14. Dorothy Sayers, *Creed or Chaos?* (London: Methuen & Co. Ltd., 1954), p. 38.

15. Ibid., p. 20.